CONVERSATION

WITH CANADIANS

Conversation with Canadians

Pierre Elliott Trudeau

FOREWORD BY IVAN L. HEAD

UNIVERSITY OF TORONTO PRESS

© this selection University of Toronto Press
Toronto and Buffalo

ISBN
casebound 0-8020-1888-2
paperback 0-8020-6147-8
microfiche 0-8020-0228-5

Printed in Canada

The excerpts from the interviews on CBC and CTV television and in
the *United Church Observer* and *Maclean's Magazine* are reproduced
with permission; that with Edith Iglauer appears with the permission
of the *New Yorker*; and those with Jay Walz and James Reston are reprin-
ted by permission of the *New York Times*.

The photographs were taken by Peter Bregg, apart from the one on
page 164 which is by Blaise Edwards. All the photographs are copy-
righted by Canadian Press.

Foreword

Pierre Elliott Trudeau has been described as a new breed of politician practising a new kind of politics – a politics of issues, not partisanship; of intelligence, not theology. His attractiveness stems from his freshness of outlook, his audacity, his intellectual honesty, and, in the words of the *Globe and Mail*, his 'capacity to communicate'.

Mr Trudeau's words combine a thoughtfulness and directness unusual for a man in high office. For that reason he is as quoted – and as cruelly misquoted – as any public figure in recent Canadian history. One example of misquotation is found in the well-known rhetorical question, 'Why should I sell your wheat?' The full passage, in which the Prime Minister answers his own question, appears within.

His speaking appearances have attracted considerable attention in the press. After hearing Mr Trudeau speak to a Parliamentary gathering in Australia, a local Member of Parliament told *Time* magazine, 'That man has done more to change the expectations Australians have of their politicians than anything else that has happened in the last ten years'. A Canberra newspaper reported that the Trudeau image 'is enhanced by the unexpected idealism and sentiment of his speeches, so beautifully worded they almost sound like poetry'. His address to the supercritical members of the National Press Club in Washington, DC, and his performance in the unrehearsed question-and-answer session that followed led a veteran American newspaperman to say to a Canadian colleague: 'I've seen a lot of them from many lands come and go but this guy comes through to me like none other'. Of the same appearance, James Reston of the *New York Times* wrote: 'Mr Trudeau had a kind of triumph ... He demonstrated that simple honesty, vivid personality and plain talk are still powerful forces in world politics ...'

The Prime Minister is perhaps at his best in the free give-and-take of press conferences, university teach-ins, and town-hall meetings. His appearances at the latter have revived them as an important political forum in Canada after more than a century of neglect and disuse, and they now form a lively technique of participatory democracy. One of Canada's veteran political reporters, W. A. Wilson of the *Montreal Star*, wrote of one of these sessions: 'Of all the speeches and question and answer sessions I have listened to over the years, I can recall none that was marked by as complete honesty as Mr Trudeau's last night... Mr Trudeau made no effort to bid for easy popularity'.

From all of these occasions and others in the period, February 1968 to February 1972, the contents of this volume have been drawn. In an effort to present as broad a selection of quotations as possible, and in order to eliminate the purely formal passages that must appear in so many addresses, this book contains speech segments, not speeches. Only two appear in their entirety, the Prime Minister's televised addresses to the nation on the occasion of the FLQ kidnapping crisis in October 1971. The criterion of selection has been to offer within these covers as broad a range of the Prime Minister's views in this turbulent and exciting period as is possible within the normal dictates of space. For the most part, the selections are arranged chronologically by topic.

IVAN L. HEAD
Ottawa
February 1972

Contents

The Human Instinct

Human dignity

We realize the inter-relationship between dignity and citizen-ship. If denied all but the bare necessities of life, if denied as well the expectation that his situation will ever improve, a human being will cease to respect the values which our society projects as the norm. In a qualitative sense such a person ceases to be a complete human being for he has been deprived of man's priceless heritage – hope. Rights and privileges demanded and exercised by others only serve to magnify to this person the desperately unfair system into which he is locked.

Material affluence is not essential to human dignity. But self-respect is. And self-respect is a product of hope and faith in the future.

University of Alberta, Edmonton, 13 May 1968

What we are trying to do in Canada is to ensure to every individual the dignity to which he as a human being is entitled. Much of the unrest and turbulence now becoming evident in Western societies originates in the belief by the young, by the poor, by the minorities, that the massive socio-economic machines that we have developed in our countries are incapable of recognizing them as persons, and of catering to their individual needs.

My government has stated again and again that it is dedica-

At Williams Lake, B C, August 1970

ted to preserving the right of every individual to do his own thing ...

We have amended our criminal laws to permit more freedom to individuals to engage in acts which, sinful though they may be or appear to many, are not possessed of that injurious quality that we normally associate with criminal conduct.

We are examining with increased vigour such debilitating side-effects of an urbanized, technological society as environmental pollution, urban housing and transportation, the protection of spaces in which to play, to think, to be free from the pressures of noise and fumes ...

If ... we are able to accomplish our goals of a better life for Canadians and at the same time demonstrate to our citizens that the social structure *is* capable of change, that it *is* sensitive to the needs and demands of individuals, that orderly processes *do* exist inside society able to act as a vehicle for the protestations and the challenges of the aggrieved, then we shall have succeeded not only for ourselves but we shall have illustrated that tribalism and withdrawal are not the answer, that diversity and non-conformity contribute to a more satisfying and culturally enriched life.

National Press Club, Washington, DC, *23 March 1969*

There is an indignity about a man out of work. There is an indignity about a man who relies upon an uncompassionate welfare system. There is an indignity about a man inadequately protected from criminal activities. Every Canadian should be able to stand tall before his children and his neighbours, and he should be able to count on governments at all levels to assist him in doing so. We do not have in Canada such a surplus of human talent that we can afford to waste the potential contribution to society of a single person. Our history books relate all too many instances of misunderstood men whose contributions were spurned because they were unorthodox, or because their attitudes and beliefs did not fit within the accepted norms of conduct of their day. We simply cannot afford the continuance of social conditions which drive men, out of a sense of frustration and futility, to the sidelines – and in some cases beyond the fringe – of legal activity. Nor are we so rich in human resources as to be able to tell anyone in this country that we have no answers to his needs, no solution to his problems.

Thomas Huxley said that 'The sense of uselessness is the severest shock which our system can sustain'. No Canadian should be regarded as useless; each must be given economic and social opportunity to attain a productive and rewarding life. Are we doing this, however, by suggesting that men who are at once talented soil analysts, practising botanists, skilled mechanics, experienced meteorologists, and shrewd commodity businessmen move to communities where there is no demand for their skills? One of the strengths of Canada has always been the responsibility and self-reliance of the Canadian farmer. This country cannot afford to regard lightly his contribution to our society. The transition necessary in some parts of Canada must be handled with sensitivity. I pledge insofar as the federal government is involved that this will be done.

We must not, for example, assume that there is some economic magic in urban living; that problems in the agricultural or fishing sectors of our economy can be solved by doing nothing more than transferring men to other, usually urban, occupations. Without question, Mr Speaker, the steady transfer of people from farm and village to city will continue, but we must not pay heed to those who argue that rural life has nothing to offer either to Canada or to persons who choose it for themselves. More is involved than economic efficiency, important as that is. There are other questions as well; questions which ask what roles are contemplated to occupy and satisfy men who for generations have been independent, self-reliant land owners; questions which enquire of the steps we are taking in our cities to provide to former farm children the same sense of responsibility and achievement that has often come to them naturally in their rural environment; questions which ask whether we are contributing to the restlessness of youth by emphasizing a social system which seems to offer them no individual challenge.

All honourable members, in the weeks since the House recessed, have travelled to their constituencies and elsewhere in

Canada. We have all had fresh opportunities to view the grandeur of this country, the pride of its people and the extent of their accomplishments: the reality that is Canada. We come back confident that we are participants in a land that is not a simple northern extension of a foreign state, not an historical accident, not a random collection of diverse persons, but a community of integrity, with its own dynamism, its own society and its own future ...

House of Commons, 24 October 1969

We also know that racial discrimination is perhaps the epitome of human indignity and that if we tolerate it even privately – in our own hearts – then we have diminished our own stature. Racism is destructive of both the perpetrator and the victim. It is evil both in its existence and its consequences. One of these consequences is violence ...

Nothing, neither treaty obligations nor political differences between nations of the most extreme sort, is adequate reason to jeopardize for our children the prospect of a world in which racial diversity is regarded as a cultural richness rather than a divisive influence. Whatever obligations we owe to our electors, they cannot outweigh in importance that responsibility to succeeding generations ... I suggest that the most important question which we should all ask ourselves is whether, conscious of the tangible and intangible values which have brought us here, we can really contemplate facing the charge which historians will put: that we failed to find some way around these problems which are uppermost in our minds today.

Commonwealth Prime Ministers' Conference, Singapore, January 1971

I think of one example of a totally destroyed, and still not identified, civilization which existed for some ten centuries prior to its overthrow in 1500 BC and which stretched from Harappa hundreds of miles down the Indus Valley to Mohenjodaro. The people lived an orderly life in well-planned and carefully laid-out cities, enjoying the benefits of drainage systems, a regulated corn supply, a rigid standard of weights and measures, and mass production of pottery.

The only fault of this great, self-sufficient civilization, it has been speculated, was its failure to adhere to a warrior philosophy. It was overthrown, plundered, and totally sacked. We would not perhaps even now know of its existence had not the engineers building the railway from Karachi to Lahore in 1856 required ballast, and discovered the brick foundations of these ancient cities. Ignominiously, the remains of this entire civilization contribute not to our knowledge of human achievement, but only to the support of a railroad. How many of us, riding in a railway carriage to Lahore, reflect on man's savagery as we rumble for hundreds of miles over brickbats of the third millennium BC?

Can we be certain that we are now on the way towards a more enlightened age? One in which men devote themselves to the betterment of their own condition, rather than the worsening of the condition of others? We are not at that point yet, anywhere. We live, it is true, in a period which permits us to construct great public works, to strive toward better techniques of food production and distribution, while at the same time enjoying the benefits of splendid architectural monuments or the wisdom of the teachings of the Prophet. But we have by no means attained an age of great wisdom. I wish that we had; a glance about this troubled planet, however, indicates that men have not yet turned their backs upon destruction. Even in my own country, as we recently had the shock of discovering, violence is no stranger.

President's Luncheon, Islamabad, Pakistan, 7 January 1971

Q The first thing I'd like to ask, Mr Prime Minister, is, are you confident that Canada is going to stay united?
A Yes, I am. I am, I guess, because I feel very deeply for Canada, and I believe most Canadians do. I am confident also for political reasons because I think that the history of the past hundred years has shown us that, by and large, the one linguistic group to whom separatism is being preached is not moved by the arguments which are used.
Q Can you think of anything that Protestant church people

in the English-speaking part of Canada may do to contribute to understanding on this whole divisive issue?

A   In specific terms I don't think I could make any suggestions, but in general terms I believe that it is because Canadians have been under the good influences of their churches that they are a tolerant people, an understanding and patient people, so that there has been little backlash against the excesses which have happened over the decades in French and in English Canada which might turn either group off. I think that there's been a remarkable show of maturity in the reaction of Canadian people, and I am sure this is because of the basic tolerance of their philosophy, a basic humanistic approach to society and equality of man.

Q   Do you think then Canadian people are reasonably free of bias or bigotry?

A   I think they are – yes.

Q   And do you feel that the churches both Protestant and Catholic are now contributing positively to unity? There have been times when they have been divisive.

A   There have been times when they were very divisive. I think that it was in periods before political pluralism was accepted as the only sane way to run a society. I think the sense of exclusivity that tended to be associated with religions in past times has now disappeared. At least it has disappeared in its political and social manifestations as far as I can see.

Q   Now, I'm going to get personal. I have been told you are a devout Catholic. I know that you don't let photographers take pictures of you going to church and apparently you don't even want it mentioned that you go to church. I don't know whether you are a devout Catholic or not, I don't know whether the people know.

A   I honestly don't know what they mean by a devout Catholic.

Q   Well, you are a believer and you go to church?

A   Yes. Does that make you a devout man?

Q   No.

A   I believe in life after death, I believe in God, and I'm a Christian.

Q   Did you ever in your youth for a time leave your faith or find yourself severely shaken in it?

A   I was shaken to the extent that people who criticized me used to say that I was Protestant more than a Catholic because I like to impose constraints on myself, but I don't like them to be imposed from the outside. You will remember that in Shaw's preface to *Saint Joan* he describes her as perhaps the first Protestant: sometimes I felt sympathy with that. I believe that the Catholic Church now would find much more accommodation for this type of person than did the particular milieu I was brought up in in school. But as to whether I had any philosophical doubts, about life and the hereafter and so on, I don't think I would like to answer that because I'm not sure how significant such doubts are. I mean, as does every young man studying philosophy, I naturally asked myself questions about the truth of all this, and about the meaning of freedom, predestination, and liberty of choice and so on. But to have asked questions of yourself about it, I think is not too important. Let's say that I remained – I remain – a believer.

Q   You were interested in finding out about the religion of other people, religions such as Buddhism and Islam on your travels: how do you react to the exclusive claims of Christianity, such as 'there is no other name under heaven whereby ye may be saved', or 'I am the way, the truth and the light; no man cometh unto the father but by me', or am I asking questions that are too personal?

A   No, that question is perfectly legitimate. I can honestly say that I have never attempted to answer that because that is not my approach to religion. In my formative years the people who influenced me most were the Christian existentialists. I mean men like Mounier and Kierkegaard and perhaps most of all Nicholas Berdyaev, and in my travels I looked for one thing more than anything. I rarely discussed, probably mainly because of language difficulties, metaphysics with the various religious people of other groups I'd meet with. But I'd very much try to see how they were incarnated, how their particular soul was incarnated or took roots into reality. I was inclined to judge the validity of a man's faith more by the depth of his roots in reality and brotherhood and love. So I felt more at home, shall we say, with some Zoroastrians in the Far East, than I did with some Catholic missionaries.

Q   Our former Moderator, Dr McClure, said some of the

Zoroastrians were the best Christian people he knew.

A Well, I never heard that but I must say that some of them I found deeply moving. This is just an example ...

Q I don't like pressing on this but you really don't like publicity about your faith. Is it a feeling that it might be exploited? Or is this just a personal thing?

A Two reasons. For one thing, it seems to me it would be pretty awful if Canadians came to choose political leaders not for their political ideas and actions, but because of their adherence or their devotedness to one faith or another. The other reason is that I feel religion is basically and essentially a communication between a man and his God and I think it is the most personal thing of all and I don't think it concerns too many people. I don't mind discussing it like this, but I do object to the sensationalism or even the voyeurism of doing things in church or out of church.

United Church Observer, *September 1971*

The just society

I am a pragmatist in politics, which does not mean that I do
not have ideals. I have some basic principles which I like to
see applied in our country and they can be very roughly and
easily defined in terms of liberty, a democratic form of government, a parliamentary system, respect of the individual,
balance between federal and provincial governments, and so
on. But beyond these ideals, I am a pragmatist, I try to find
the solution for the present situation, and I do not feel myself
bound by any doctrines or any rigid approaches to any of
these problems.
Canadian Club, Winnipeg, 23 May 1968

The increasing sophistication of the electorate relates also to
young people. Marshall McLuhan has helped us all to realize
a lot of things in this area; how a child of three or four learns
things on television which we learned only when we were 18
or 19. I'm not thinking necessarily of events, I'm thinking
of images. They see pictures of fighting and dying. They are
aware of wars abroad and great events happening everywhere
in the world.

Young people today are much more sophisticated in political terms than we were at their age. This sophistication has led
them to want to participate to a much greater degree. I often
think the term 'drop-out' as it is applied to many of our youth
is exactly the wrong one. They are not dropping out, they are
dropping in on society. They are letting us know they want to

have a part in this world and in the decisions that order the world and their destinies.

In this sense, I'm very concerned about the role youth will be playing. It is extremely important that those in authority – whether it be in the state or in the university or in the home or in the corporations – keep up a dialogue with young people so that the values they are developing for themselves do not develop in isolation but are constantly being tested against the values in which we believe.

Answers to questions by Charles Templeton, Maclean's Magazine, *3 April 1969*

If you make promises, that gives you obligations that you have to carry out. I was afraid of those obligations. You mortgage yourself and lose the freedom of decision. Justice is the problem – the one about which I have been concerned the most, stated the most, thought the most. I guess most of the authors I've read crystallize my particular idea of virtue – that justice is a cornerstone of the society I live in, the basis of all human relations in the family or the state. I was not dreaming the Just Society up as a catchword or cliché, and I shrink from that thought now. To me, it summed up the total of the relationships in a society of free men. The Just Society is the kind of society freedom would establish. Looking ahead, I don't think a state can say, 'Here's a state, a package imposed on you'. A Just Society is one toward which every citizen must work, and the first condition of such a society is that of respecting the liberty of individuals.

Interview with Edith Iglauer, New Yorker, *5 July 1959*

We have all watched with a mixture of admiration and concern the criticism of young Canadians for the shortcomings of the society they are inheriting: criticism of the difficulties which face our native people; criticism of laws which in their application discriminate against the weak and the ignorant; of an international community which accepts death and destruction as normal; of parliamentary and governmental institutions which do not respond to the needs of Canadians as well as they should. These criticisms have been aired not only in a random, unstructured fashion but as well, fortunately, through the political institutions which are the vehicles of change in democratic societies. Every one of us in this House must be committed to the success of involving young Canadians in the political life of this country.

Let me repeat this government's concern for what it regards as Canada's two most valuable assets, Mr Speaker: its human resources and its natural resources. It is in terms of husbanding and nourishing those resources that this government views every problem. What we do, or fail to do, in the course of this administration will, I hope, be measured in that light. I invite honourable members to regard the current legislation programme in the same terms. This invitation is issued because I am conscious of the fact that day-to-day decisions concerning day-to-day crises may often appear to be unpopular. It is inevitable in a country as vast as Canada, with interests as manifold as ours, that all Canadians will not always agree on assessments, on responses, or on priorities. Nevertheless, those assessments, those responses, and those priorities will, I pledge, always be consistent in the long run with certain principles:
– we will not barter a clean and wholesome environment for industrial or commercial growth, and call it progress;
– we will not substitute privacy and other individual freedoms with a ubiquitous government and call it either efficiency or social welfare;
– we will not in this country permit bigotry to replace tolerance, violence to replace dialogue, or discrimination to replace moderation, and excuse it all in the name of freedom of expression.

House of Commons, 24 October 1969

Q Mr Trudeau, I would like to ask you about your Indian policy. Why do you insist on integrating the Indian into Canadian society when he doesn't want to be integrated? Even you, yourself, have suggested that we live in an unjust society, there's poverty, pollution, slums. Why do you want to make them like that?
A We're not really forcing them to integrate. We're not for-

cing anyone to do anything. That is why we published a policy paper, you could call it a white paper on Indians ... What we say essentially is this: Canada is at a crossroads; the Canadian Indian has to choose and the white Canadian has to choose too. For a hundred years and more, they have not been integrated; they have been living apart, they have been under special laws, they didn't come under provincial jurisdiction, they came under special treatment by a special department of the federal government. They lived on reserves; they didn't have the right to sell their land; they were not equals in our society. And what we are saying essentially is this: if you want to remain this way, fine; if you want to stay in reserves, if you want to not integrate – to use your word – if you want to remain apart as a race within Canada, as a nation within a nation, we won't force you. But we are telling you you have to make the choice now. And we're telling you that the way we see the history of Canada and of the western nations developing, no small group of people can long remain outside of the mainstream of education, technology, urban living, and all these things (some of which have produced pretty awful results, I agree). You cannot do this without paying a very heavy penalty in terms of the health of children, the education of minds, the freedom to move, the right to accumulate property and the right to be treated as an equal under the law. We are just saying to the Indians, you've got a choice now and we're putting this position to you ...

I remember this very type of audience during an election campaign saying, when are we going to do away with this special treatment for Indians, when are we going to make them one of us, equal to us so they have a right to integrate into our society. Well, we said, here's a policy which would permit you to do it. It's going to be tough and it's going to take long, but we'll help you if you want. And it will only work if the white people in Canada, the other people, agree to help you do this. But if you people don't want – those of you who are not Indians – if you don't want it to happen and if the Indian people don't want it to happen, it won't happen. The Indians will continue living on land which is held in trust by the federal government; they'll continue coming under the jurisdiction of a particular department; they won't be equal citi-

zens to the other citizens. And this is the choice and we're not
forcing it on anybody. But before rejecting it, you should ask
yourselves about the alternatives. There is a lot of emotion-
alism in this too. It's easy to reject the defects in our society
and say they will come in with us and they will be poor and so
on. But they're poor now.

Q   They are afraid though that integration will lead to assimi-
lation – cultural genocide they call it. Do you agree with that?

A   Well, there are two ways of disappearing. One is to lock
yourself up in a ghetto behind walls and sort of stand fast,
protected by these walls of the law or of your ghetto or of your
reservation, and if you do this you risk some chance that the
caravan of humanity will not attack you in your fortress but
they will walk on to the plains of time and they will be on
somewhere in the future ... There are many minorities in Canada which have chosen to integrate into our society. It doesn't
mean they lost all their values; it doesn't mean that they can't
preserve a certain number of things. But they have a choice.
In a sense, to a very different degree, this is the choice we
have in Quebec and this is why I am for integration into the
Canadian federation – because there is a way of separating
Quebec and of saying we will be more protected if we don't
have to work with others and if we exist *entre nous* and if you
leave us alone. It's a view which is an acceptable view, but it's
not mine. And I don't think that it is the long-run view and the
enlightened view of the Indians and the white people in Canada. But if this is what they want, it's fine. We will keep the
Indians in ghettos as long as they want.

CBC-TV *'Under Attack', Carleton University, Ottawa*
24 February 1970

I am so happy wherever I can to meet students – the reception
is not always so warm and hospitable as this one. The reason
why I do like to meet them ... is that there is something happening in the seventies in industrial societies as we see them
developing, which has two mainsprings which are perhaps
completely new. The first is the cybernetic aspect of the technological revolution and the second is ... there is a particular
characteristic of the young people today: it's that they are un-

censored or unprogrammed to a degree which I believe no other generation before has been uncensored. Until now we have all received our values from our parents, or from our church or our families or our schools or our universities, and we either kept them or rejected or modified them – and there has always been the fathers-and-sons conflict – but it was always based on something we had received from others, as a superego or as a universal morality, whereas now I think for the first time in industrial societies ... people today receive their values from their peers. Young people learn values from television, cinema and radio as early as they learn from their parents and as early as they receive them very often from their church. From three or four years on the child is tuned in, plugged in to events happening halfway across the world and he knows them as soon as his parents do and sometimes sooner. And I think this has created a tremendous force, a force for renovation in our societies, and I hasten to add I do not think that it makes young people always right. I think they are as often wrong as previous generations were, and I am not one of those who has a particular reverence or veneration for youth. But I do feel that there is perhaps more to learn now from youth than previously, because experience has no longer the same value. The events in the world of today are changing to a much greater degree and with much more rapidity than they have in the past ... The rapidity of the new facts developing calls for perhaps a set of new values and because you are unprogrammed by previous moralists to a large extent I believe that you can help us to discover values for a better society. And this explains, I think, to a large degree the preoccupation of young people in universities in particular with the quality of life rather than quantities. In my generation and generations before, linear thinking dominated all our definitions of progress. If we had more automobiles and more social legislation, if we had more frigidaires and televisions and more taxes and more universities and more houses, you know it is a better society. But we are discovering now – pollution and so on – that this isn't necessarily so. Well, the danger with unprepared speeches is that they can go on and on. I'll sit down and listen to questions.

Q Mr Prime Minister, you stated in an earlier press conference that in your opinion youth is beginning to think of the quality of life rather than, say, material gain coupled with greed and territorial exploitation as the result. But the growing tendency amongst many of the politically potent sections of my age group is to think the world is for the young and if the older generations will not change to save the world then they will take control. I think this trend became evident in the French revolution in '68 and in the growing rebellion in America. How do you see your role in relation to youth? I ask this because many psychologists point to the possibility of a technological and social revolution in the future if the older generations do not acquiesce.

A ... In Canada there is a recognition, I think, if not of the greater maturity at least of the greater awareness of youth and the greater desire of youth to participate in the shaping of the destinies of the society in which they live. Now, can I be more specific? If you are talking of representation, I agree there should be a great deal of it. We tend to encourage as much as possible the awareness of young people by inviting them to enter the various political parties in Canada. We believe that the great danger would be that young people cop out or drop out, feeling that governments are irrelevant, that they are not honest, and that you really can't trust them or that you can't get the right things done through them. This of course is, to me, a wrong solution. By dropping out you renounce the possibility of shaping the destiny of your society. I believe you should drop in, and I believe it's up to parties and governmental structures to facilitate this. In other words, I'd rather, on occasions such as this and others, have the young people in our society give their governments hell, or their authorities or their establishments hell, in order that they feel that they can get their point of view at least understood if not accepted, than have them out invading administration buildings or marching on parliament or setting fire to research centres. In other words, I believe the tremendous amount of energy which is contained in the young people today, the numbers of young people in our societies who are involved in the education process, is so great that something has to give somewhere ...

In front of the Legislature Building, Winnipeg, July 1969

You know, there is this tremendous amount of physical, of sexual, of spiritual energy which is bottled up in educational institutions for ten, fifteen, twenty years, thirty years sometimes, depending on how many degrees you want to get, and this is basically an unnatural process. Mankind was not created this way. The people with all those pent-up energies, beginning with the oncoming of puberty until the time when they can eventually get married and earn their living and raise a family – there is something unnatural about it and I think it is extremely important, if the machine isn't going to explode, it is extremely important to make sure this energy can find its outlets. And for many of them the outlet can be essentially spiritual or intellectual, and we all know about the theories of sublimation and so on. But let's face it, many students are not all researchers, and they're not all intellectuals, and in the democratization of our education processes many more people have been brought into the educational institutions than are able to sublimate their energies in research, whether it be in laboratories or libraries and so on. So there's all this energy and some of it can go to waste and some of it could destroy the very institutions themselves. We have to come to grips with this problem. You know, it's an organic, it's a genetic problem, and I think this aspect has not often enough been considered as has been the simple physiological force. And it's for this reason that there is so much disorder I think in the multi-universities, and it's for this reason – getting back to your question – there has to be much greater participation at all levels by students so that their energies can be channelled into creative processes.

I'll try to be more brief in my answers.

'Teach-In', Australian National University, Canberra, Australia, 18 May 1970

[Indian equality was] an election issue not created by us or indeed only by you but by the Canadian people. I think it is something which has come to the surface of the conscience of the Canadian people. We realize that, for a hundred years, generally not because of ill will, but because of, as you say in your red paper, perhaps a lack of understanding or of ignorance, or lack of an occasion to come to grips with the problem – but we do realize that the issue of Indian rights is very much on the conscience of the Canadian people and that it has to be solved.

And that is why one of the very first priorities of the government which was elected after that campaign was to appoint a minister – and a young minister who also belonged to a minority in Canada and who had no prejudices and who honestly didn't think he was up to the job, but who had courage and determination and who had no vested interests in any particular solution – we asked him to come to grips with this problem and to come to grips quickly with it ... We came up with a policy proposal. We said the Canadian people, not only the Indian people, but the Canadian people are at a crossroads, that we have to decide now where we're going; if we don't take some steps it may be another hundred years before we come to grips with the problem. So let's do something which may not be perfect, which may not be final, but which is in the way of a proposal, a suggestion, so that Canadians, not only Indian Canadians, but all Canadians can come to face with this problem ...

Well, now the next phase has arrived, the phase where the Indian people have looked at this and they have said, it's not good. And I'm sure that we were very naive in some of the statements we made in the paper. We had perhaps the prejudices of small 'l' liberals, and white men at that, who thought that equality meant the same law for everybody, and that's why as a result of this we said, 'Well, let's abolish the Indian Act and make Indians citizens of Canada like everyone else. And let's let Indians dispose of their lands just like every other Canadian. And let's make sure that Indians can get their rights, education, health and so on, from the governments like every other Canadian.' But we have learnt in the process that perhaps we were a bit too theoretical, we were a bit too abstract, we were not, as Mr Cardinal suggests, perhaps pragmatic enough or understanding enough, and that's fine. We are here to discuss this.

You have said yourselves it would take time; it will take time. You said it is a difficult problem; it's obviously a difficult problem. We can't in one year undo the injustices or misunderstandings of a hundred or two hundred years of history, and certainly we can't do it alone. And that's why we

have these meetings and that's why we'll have many more ...
*Meeting with the Indian Association of Alberta and the National
Indian Brotherhood, Ottawa, 4 June 1970*

We have been reminded in recent days that the violence which
is now so familiar to so many countries is no stranger to Canada. We have seen evidence in Canada this past summer of
challenges to some of our most cherished concepts. We have
been told by some that the air that we have so long believed to
be as free as any in the world, that the equality which we
thought was so widespread in practice, that the simple tolerance and goodwill of one Canadian to another – that these
beliefs and these criteria are misleading or false. We are challenged and we must respond. The response cannot be a forfei-
ture of our values, but it must include a sincere attempt to ensure that all Canadians have available to them effective ave-
nues for social change and political action. It must include as
well, however, an expression of our strong belief that liberty
and anarchy are contradictory, that democracy and violence
cannot co-exist, that our freedom is dependent upon wise restraints.

If Canadians are unable to pursue a system of peaceful resolution of problems, then what persons are? If we, who associate one with the other within a framework as flexible as is federalism, who are predisposed to tolerance, and who enjoy the
benefits of linguistic and cultural differences – if we still depart from reason, then surely we are in no position to criticize
other countries for their social difficulties.

I believe that we can profit from the knowledge that violence begets violence, that the experience of man demonstrates
with blinding clarity that in a jungle all are not equal, but all
are vulnerable.

Freedom and liberty are neither gained nor retained without cost. The cost takes the form of a burden which demands
of us all the human elements of responsibility, trust, and common sense: responsibility, because every Canadian is a partici-
pant in the democratic process; trust to promote reasonable,
reasoned argument; common sense to enable us to see what is,
and what is not, possible and desirable.
House of Commons, 9 October 1970

Who of you at this moment are saying to yourselves, 'Women! why doesn't he speak on an important subject?'

One of the most heartening and exciting aspects of our age is the willingness and the desire of people, and especially of young people, to look at old problems in different perspectives and to approach conventional wisdom and attitudes with a refreshing and questioning candour. This challenge to convention is apparent in many areas; it is, for example, causing us all to reconsider the manner in which we regard the role of women in a modern community. It should cause us to question the social effects and liabilities of traditional attitudes.

It helps to recall how iniquitous was the legal position in Canada of women even a few years ago. In 1928, a date well within the lifetime of many in this room, the Supreme Court of Canada was still able to interpret the word 'persons' in the British North America Act as not including women for purposes of appointment to the Senate. If ever a reply were needed to the often-voiced male contention that women themselves have chosen their limitations, then this is surely it: that the highest court in the land could decide solemnly in the year 1928 that women are not, under the constitution of Canada, persons.

Changes have of course come but they have come ever so slowly. It has been 55 years since the franchise was first extended to women in Canada (in Manitoba); yet in that entire interval only two women have served in federal cabinets, and today, of 264 members in the House of Commons, only one is a woman. Indeed, in the half-century between 1920 and 1970 only eighteen women have been elected to Parliament.

It was in 1916 that Emily Murphy was appointed by the government of Alberta as the first woman to hold judicial office in Canada, yet in the 55 years since that event only one woman has been seated on the bench of a superior court in the entire country (in Quebec in 1969).

Perhaps this generation has recognized as past generations have not that discrimination based upon sexual or racial reasons lasts for a lifetime. There are, after all, only two permanent conditions attributable to human beings. One is sex. The other is race. All other distinctions from which discrimination may grow are temporary in nature or are subject to change. Education, religion, language, age, health, economic stature, experience – all are or can be transient. Discrimination based upon sex or racial origin is thus doubly unfair. The person against whom the discrimination is practised had no choice of origin and has no option of change.

For the same reason, because of this permanence of condition, none of us – men or women – is able totally to understand the view of the other sex. It is impossible in this realm for either of us to perceive objectively; none of us can remove ourselves from our bastion and look in from a neutral vantage point. Yet we must try; we must begin to try. Unless we overcome these barriers to understanding we are less than we might be – less than we should be. Society cannot become mature without the full participation of women. Society will not become mature without a sharing of experience.

In mechanics, when two equal and parallel but opposite forces are applied to the two ends of a lever, they are said to form a couple, a dynamic system.

The basic forces in society obey similar laws. The two elements that compose society – men and women – form a couple, or system, of forces, even at the group level. When these forces are combined, their efforts are multiplied, and acquire new and previously unsuspected dimensions. Together but different, equal but distinct, men and women can discover each other, can have a mutually creative influence on each other, and can thenceforth discover and create an infinitely more exciting and fruitful world than they could acting independently.

Participation in human activity by women is therefore not only valuable, but indispensable.

Some of the barriers are of recent origin; others have beginnings shrouded in the dimness of early history; some are the product of male chauvinism; still others are rooted in social patterns that have remained distinct and viable from century to century. Each category requires separate appraisal. The concept of the family unit, for example, has resisted change in almost every society in every country in every age of recorded history. Certain skills are required in the raising of children, certain functions demand to be performed. The nominee to supply these skills and perform these functions need not be determined by a sexual qualification, but equally these skills and these functions cannot be overlooked or rejected in our desire to overcome the shortcomings of the past. The role of the family and the place of children must be examined at the same time as we examine the role of adult persons.

This does not assume a 'place' for women; it accepts distinctive contributions. The challenge should be to accept distinction through accommodation, not to petrify it through discrimination.

Are we right in assuming, for example, as so many persons now do, that employment, rather than occupation or contribution, is the primary criterion of usefulness; that motherhood and the education of children is not a task as important, as challenging and fulfilling as any in the world? I am sure we are not. Are we not remiss in our oft-repeated failure to recognize spontaneously and more enthusiastically the immense contribution to society made by women through their participation in volunteer activities? At the same time are we confident that our society could not become more rewarding – perhaps even more productive – if it dropped its insistence on standard 40-hour work-weeks and permitted variable work schedules to many women who have some time, much talent and considerable incentive? Are we even aware of the range of rich benefits that we deny ourselves by restricting so severely and casting so rigidly relations between men and women? Do we think of one another as persons?

In sexual discrimination, as in racial discrimination, the stature of the person discriminating suffers as much as that of the person discriminated against. Both persons are losers in the process.

And the society is the loser as well. The entire community is denied the contributions of large numbers of women in capacities that we in Canada for decades have regarded as masculine preserves. There is no evidence, for example, that the standards of health care in the Soviet Union, or the durability of Soviet bridges, are less than what they might be because of the large – in one instance overwhelming – number of women in the medical and engineering professions. There is no evidence that the people of India, of Ceylon, of Israel are less well served by governments headed by female prime ministers than would be the case had men retained those offices. Indeed from my own recent meetings with Prime Ministers Gandhi, Bandaranaike and Meir, I would suggest that the evidence is quite the other way. Yet in Canada we have permitted ourselves to develop attitudes which are hostile to the reception of women into a number of professions and trades and into politics. In the result each one of us, men and women, is demeaned.

Until Canada is given the opportunity of utilizing to the full the offerings of all Canadians, this country and the people who live in it will not gain fulfilment. We cannot assume that the contribution of women will be a mere extension of or even support for the contribution of men. Their performance will not only be original; it will be sometimes competitive and sometimes complementary. We have no means of perceiving the dimensions of their offering; we know only that it will be rich, that it will be persuasive, and that it will enhance our society and all who live in it. It is an exciting prospect.

Convention, ignorance, fear, lassitude, acquiescence, and even prejudice – these and other factors have combined for centuries to deny to women equal opportunity to choose without restriction their own careers and to develop without discrimination their own abilities. Society has paid a heavy price for these policies. Part of the price is reflected in the fact that there is still no force strong enough to overcome instantly such an accumulation of attitudes. Yet there is ample force to disclose the heavy toll in unused human potential which is the product of these attitudes. And fortunately it is this force which is now being brought to bear in the form of thoughtful studies which reveal the cost of our past, and the penalty which we shall pay in the future unless we change, and change rapidly.

Toronto & District Liberal Association, 3 March 1971

The government believes as well that youth is sincere in its efforts to improve society and that young people are anxious to work and to engage in activities which are intended to make Canada a better place in which to live. The government proposes therefore to encourage young persons to direct their energy, their imagination and their altruism into projects which are beneficial to the entire community. The Opportunities for Youth Program will combine the resources of the government with the resourcefulness of youth. We are saying, in effect, to the youth of Canada that we are impressed by their desire to fight pollution; that we believe they are well motivated in their concern for the disadvantaged; that we have confidence in their value system. We are also saying that we intend to challenge them to see if they have the stamina and self-discipline to follow through on their criticism and advice.
House of Commons, 16 March 1971

Man's technical achievements in the past two hundred years have been breathtaking, but the test of our civilization will be the measure of control to which these achievements are required to submit in order to be at the service of society. Unquestionably, the speed of our accomplishments appears to have outdistanced our ability to fit our technological triumphs within some framework of reason. Is this a permanent condition? Surely not, for if it were, the future of mankind would be doubtful indeed. What has happened is that in the undisciplined progression of events, the unpredictable leaps and bounds of technical knowledge passed long ago the rationale for its wise application and use. We stand at this juncture in history in as great a need of a philosophy of technology as did the world in the seventeenth century need a philosophy of science and mathematics just prior to Descartes' *Discourse on Method*.

In the absence of a philosophy of this age we must give the appearance of a generation gone mad. Or is it that we are just so busy looking for a parking place that we have no time to be anything but indifferent to what is happening about us?

Surely we are not so ignorant as to assume that, somehow,

the earth will begin producing more resources at an inexhaustible rate. Surely we do not prefer to live beside garbage dumps, to breathe smog, and to look out on polluted oceans. Do we really believe that a high standard of living involves daily traffic jams and ear-splitting noise levels? Are we totally indifferent to the world in which our children and grandchildren will be forced to live? Have we, in short, permitted our common sense and our value system both to be so distorted that we equate 'good' with 'consumption' and 'quality' with 'growth'? ...

Perhaps I am too critical. Perhaps we are caught up in a spiral of circumstance in which our desire for jobs and decent incomes and variety in our lives provides us with no alternative except to lay waste the surface of the earth and to foul the atmosphere. After all, how can one measure the value of a salmon stream, or a species of wildlife, against the benefits of an open-pit mine which will provide jobs for hundreds? How can one compare the pleasures of untouched wilderness with the convenience of a four-lane highway? We seem to have so much untouched space; why not use some of it for people?

There are no easy answers to these questions for the problems they pose are in many instances contradictory. But that does not mean there are no answers, or that mankind in the past has been unable to come to grips with equally trying dilemmas. Some solutions have been superior to others, in large measure because a sense of wonder and awe has been permitted to exist beside the regimentation of reason, to prevent what Kenneth Clark describes as 'a new form of barbarism' resulting from the 'triumph of rational philosophy'.
Liberal Party of Vancouver, 1 May 1971

The Canada of 1871 was by no means assured of a brilliant, or indeed any, future. The annexation movement was still alive and in 1886 a bill would be introduced into the United States Congress designed to facilitate the entry into the United States of the Canadian provinces and the western territories.

The uncertain future of Canada was taken in stride by your predecessors. It was regarded as one more factor to be taken into account in addition to all the other unknowns which have been accepted as a part of business since the days of the earliest merchants in pre-Biblical times; another of the many risks inherent in any trading operation. Businessmen have never shied away from this type of uncertainty for in it lies the adventure, the opportunity, the challenge and the rewards which are the essential and attractive elements of business.

There is another kind of uncertainty abroad today, however. An uncertainty which is becoming more pervasive as time goes on and which contributes a substantial factor of doubt to the future not just of this, but of most other western countries; an uncertainty which presents a new dimension of risk to the businessman and for which he is no more adequately prepared than is any other member of society. This uncertainty is not aimed at the business community and it is surely not inspired by government. It is a product of our times. It is a reflection of the growing demand of people – largely in North America, in Europe, in Australasia, and in Japan – that all human activity should contribute to the well-being of society as a whole.

Questions are being asked about the value of our economic and social accounting procedures; about the proper social roles of industry, of government, of the individual; about the relationship of work to leisure, of the environment to human activity, of societal structure to individual need. Were one of our forebears of a century ago – be he industrialist or politician – to return to the world of today he would not merely be confused; he would probably comment as did General Cornwallis when the British Army was defeated by George Washington and his revolutionary forces: he said, 'The world is turned upside down'.

Every Canadian is affected by this kind of uncertainty. If we seize the opportunity which it presents to us, however, every Canadian will benefit. The demands for social or human benefit are not a quirk of this government; they reflect a widespread belief that Canadians possess the space, the resources, the ability, the technology and – above all – the common sense to create and preserve a society of tolerance, of understanding, and of beauty, with a fair distribution of wealth which permits all persons to live in dignity. What is new in all this is not only a value system with a changed emphasis, but as

well the determination that the system shall be implemented.
What is new is the demand that government and industry
refine and reform where necessary in order to permit society
to meet these value goals.

Canadian Manufacturers' Association, Toronto, 8 June 1971

Q How do you feel about the young people, especially those
youngsters hitchhiking around the country? You are concerned about those who couldn't get jobs, but how about those
who are doing this instead of taking a job – how do you feel
about them?

A I think it's great. I think that more and more young people
are discovering that gainful employment isn't the only thing in
life. That they can perhaps be just as useful to society and
themselves by travelling across the land or around the world,
learning more about humanity and going through the various
experiences which will make their adulthood more productive.

Q You did that when you were a young man. How productive was it for you from the point of view of education and understanding of the world? Was it equal to a year or two in college?

A Oh, gosh, I suppose it was probably equal to ten years in
college in terms of seeing the world, understanding people,
feeling misery and poverty and isolation at first hand, and also
probably in the moulding of my own personality. You remember in Melville's *Moby Dick* I believe it was Ishmael who said
that when he feels that desire to go out and knock men's hats
off, he realizes it's time to go to sea, and he hunts the white
whale. I think young people are like that all the time. I think I
was much better advised to bum around the world for a few
years than to stay around Canada knocking people's hats off.
And I think a lot of the young people today are realizing that.
You know you have a lot of impatience with reality as you see
it when you're a young man and full of dynamism and
strength and ideals and so on. I think it's good that you test
the reality that surrounds you in your neighbourhood with the
reality as it is in other parts of the world; you come up with a
better judgment. I'm not meaning that literally you can only

do that and not go to school at all but in terms of enrichment of a personality I think it's a fabulous thing. I'm told now that you must find farther and farther away places. I remember when I went to Kabul or to Khartoum or to Nepal, there were no other bums around, if I can use that expression, but today I suppose there are great colonies of hippies in such places, and that's a pity.

Q Should we have a floor under which no man may sink even if it's his own fault? Should every Canadian be given a basic income whether he works or not?

A I think my answer would be to state what I think is theoretically right and then what is practically possible. If a man is young and healthy, society should not give him a basic income. He should not be given dole. He should not be eligible for welfare. If he can work and if there is work available, he should take his choice. If he wants to be a hermit or beggar, that's fine. If he wants to move with the sun and live off the land, that's fine. If he is in a society which has work for him, I don't think he should theoretically be eligible for welfare. But, in practice, the administration of these laws would be difficult; to examine each person and say, 'are you physically ill, or are you psychologically deranged, or are you just going through a phase now where you will be stricken by disease and blight if you're not fed, and therefore we must help you?' Because of the impossibility of going through this type of exercise I don't see any easy way of disqualifying people on the basis that they decide not to work. Every time I have a political rally I meet some people who say, 'I need a job'. I met one yesterday and I said, 'What is your trade? What would you like to work at? Do you want a job?' I told him, 'I'll find you a job'. And he said, 'I want a hundred thousand jobs. Canada needs a hundred thousand jobs'. He didn't want a job, he was just demonstrating. More power to him. If he doesn't want a job, let him wander. He's a young man and perhaps it's his time to do so. If he wants a job then I think we should help him find one. If we can't help him find one then I think we should take care of him because society is responsible for its social organization, and if it can't provide the wherewithal for

men to be gainfully employed then it should pay the penalty
and give them welfare.
United Church Observer, September 1971

A policy of multiculturalism within a bilingual framework
commends itself to the government as the most suitable means
of assuring the cultural freedom of Canadians. Such a policy
should help to break down discriminatory attitudes and cultural jealousies. National unity if it is to mean anything in the
deeply personal sense, must be founded on confidence in one's
own individual identity; out of this can grow respect for that
of others and a willingness to share ideas, attitudes and assumptions. A vigorous policy of multiculturalism will help
create this initial confidence. It can form the base of a society
which is based on fair play for all.

The government will support and encourage the various
cultures and ethnic groups that give structure and vitality to
our society. They will be encouraged to share their cultural
expression and values with other Canadians and so contribute
to a richer life for us all.
House of Commons, 8 October 1971

Canada's population distribution has now become so balanced
as to deny to any one racial or linguistic component an absolute majority. Every single person in Canada is now a member
of a minority group. Linguistically, our origins are one third
English, one third French, and one third neither. We have no
alternative but to be tolerant of one another's differences. Beyond the threshold of tolerance, however, we have countless
opportunities to benefit from the richness and variety of a Canadian life which is the result of this broad mix. The fabric of
Canadian society is as resilient as it is colourful. It is a multi-
cultural society; it offers to every Canadian the opportunity to
fulfil his own cultural instincts and to share those from other
sources. This mosaic pattern, and the moderation which it includes and encourages, makes Canada a very special place.

It is a special place, and a stronger place as well. Each of
the many fibres contributes its own qualities and Canada gains

strength from the combination. We become less like others; we become less susceptible to cultural, social or political envelopment by others. We become less inclined – certainly less obliged – to think in terms of national grandeur; inclined not at all to assume a posture of aggressiveness, or ostentation, or might. Our image is of a land of people with many differences – but many contributions, many variations in view – but a single desire to live in harmony. We have concluded in Canada almost without debate that true greatness is not measured in terms of military might or economic aggrandisement. On a planet of finite size, the most desirable of all characteristics is the ability and desire to cohabit with persons of differing backgrounds, and to benefit from the opportunities which this offers.

To those who argue – as some still do – that cultural differences are divisive and weakening, that Canada would be less susceptible to internal dissension if we were all of the same mould, I respond with an emphatic denial. Uniformity is neither desirable nor possible in a country the size of Canada. We should not even be able to agree upon the kind of Canadian to choose as a model, let alone persuade most people to emulate it. There are surely few policies potentially more disastrous for Canada than to tell all Canadians that they must be alike. There is no such thing as a model or ideal Canadian. What could be more absurd than the concept of an 'all-Canadian' boy or girl? A society which emphasizes uniformity is one which creates intolerance and hate. A society which eulogizes the average citizen is one which breeds mediocrity.

What the world should be seeking and what we in Canada must continue to cherish, are not concepts of uniformity but human values: compassion, love and understanding. Our standard in all activities should be one of excellence, but our routes to its achievement may be as numerous as there are Canadians who pursue it.

Languages have two functions. They act both as a vehicle of communication, and as a preservation of culture. Governments can support languages in either or both of these roles, but it is only in the communication role that the term 'official' is employed. An overwhelming number of Canadians use

At Repulse Bay, NWT, March 1970

either English or French in their day-to-day communications with one another and with government. It is for this practical reason – not some rationalization about founding races – that these two languages have attained an official character in Canada. French and English are not superior to or more precise than any other language. They are simply used more in Canada.

The other use of language, as an ingredient of cultural preservation, as the vehicle for the dissemination and inheritance of literary and artistic treasures, requires no official recognition. Language in this sense is a contributor of those values which guarantee to Canada its diversity, its richness, its strength. Language so described becomes synonymous with culture. Though language for that purpose need not be official, it nevertheless deserves the support of government. A Royal Commission recommended almost two years ago that that support should take the form of specific acts of assistance, including financial help. In the intervening months the federal government has pondered how best those recommendations could be implemented, has discussed them with other levels of government and with representatives of the several ethnic communities, and has constructed much of the infra-structure needed for the day when such support could commence.

Mr Chairman, I am happy to be able to confirm to this audience of members of Canada's fifth largest cultural community that that day has arrived.

As I announced in the House of Commons yesterday, the Government of Canada has approved all of the recommendations of Book IV of the Royal Commission on Bilingualism and Biculturalism as they apply to the federal jurisdiction. In fact, in some respects we have gone further.

Ukrainian-Canadian Congress, Winnipeg, 9 October 1971

Q   Mr Trudeau, how do you feel about abortions and the legalization of them to the extent that it is left up to the individual?

A   This is a question I find great difficulty in answering with satisfaction. If you permit me, I will just remind you very briefly what we did two years ago in Parliament. We amended the Criminal Code to permit legal abortions in hospitals when it's approved by a therapeutic abortion committee and when the committee says that the health or the life of the mother is endangered. So we made substantial progress at least by permitting doctors to give abortions legally in certain conditions. It was done, as you know, in spite of the fact that it divided the country very badly. We had a filibuster in Parliament to prevent that and other amendments to the Criminal Code going through ... My memory is that it took a total of something like six weeks in the House of Commons in order to get that amendment, which is certainly not half as far as you would like, through the House of Commons. So my estimate is that it would not be possible to get the kind of amendment you say through the House of Commons, certainly not now but even earlier in the next session without spending many many weeks on it. And even if we did not I could not even guarantee that it would pass because, even though we have a majority in Parliament, this is a question which divides people very deeply according to their conscience and it is more than likely that many of them would refuse to vote on party lines. Therefore I see no circumstance in which we could, within the next little while, pass the kind of law you are suggesting. We did make a commitment that the subject would be debated in Parliament, and it will as soon as we can find time for it, in order to test opinion of Parliamentarians and to see perhaps if my assumptions are wrong. If we feel that there is a great chance, from the short debate we will have, to get the law through quickly, either going as far as you say or less far or in a different direction, then we will consider introducing it. But once again my guess from the last experience is that a much smaller amendment took weeks and weeks and weeks and that this major amendment would not only take weeks and months but it probably would not even pass. I probably should stop there and say that's the answer – certainly wiser politically. But you may want to know what I feel personally about it ...

Q That's what I wanted to know.

A Why do you want to know that?

Q You don't have to answer it.

A I don't feel that I can speak with great authority on this mainly because I am not a woman ... Really in this case I think that it should be essentially the women who would have the louder say in this because they are the ones who are carrying the foetus, they are the ones who are victimized by bad abortions, they are the ones who have to take the very frightening moral decisions of killing something which is living inside them. So I can only react as a man and I can only react by giving you my very general philosophy on it. There are some cases – even assuming that the foetus is a child and that it is a living thing and that abortion is murder of it, or shall we say abortion is killing of a living thing, even assuming this – I say there are some circumstances in which killing a living thing is, though horrible to think of, it is in my morality permissible. And I guess it is in most people's morality, because there are, you know, when there is a war, there are killings; I don't agree with those any more than anything else. But when it is legitimate defence and somebody is trying to kill you, you fight – damn hard and you may kill him. So I accepted, we accepted, that principle in our amendment. We said there are some cases where you can kill a foetus, assuming it is a living thing, to save the mother's life or even to save her health as judged by a committee of doctors ...

Now quite frankly that's as far as I want to go. But once again here I was really very influenced by the overwhelming feeling of women on this, because they are the ones who are making the terrible moral decision of killing. And I don't envy them for it. I think it is a terribly difficult moral question, a human question, and I know the ladies, the women, are very severely divided. We have Women's Lib and the Royal Commission on the Status of Women advocating greater liberalization of the laws, but we have hundreds and thousands of representations from women's leagues in the other direction saying that they cannot condone this. So if there were a debate in Parliament, these are the things I would say and I would especially listen to women's opinions on this and hope that they will arrive at some consensus. On balance you know if there is a doubt I prefer giving a chance to life rather than to killing, but it is not I who is carrying the child.

Question and Answer Session, Prince Edward High School, Dartmouth, NS, 29 October 1971

You don't protect a language essentially by laws or even by a constitution. You can prop it up artificially that way but if you want to have a language preserved and have it flourish, it will be by making that language, in a sense, the expression of a dynamic, lively, important, cultured, wealthy, powerful group. I don't think you do this by laws. You can't legislate a language into importance. You can, once again, make sure that the people who speak a language become a very important contributor to the society in which they live and therefore that language will take prominence.

Mount Royal Liberal Association, Montreal, 25 November 1971

Q If it is true, as most people seem to be saying these days, that allegiance to the church and even to belief in secular institutions like the university and the press, has declined, then where is the moral leadership of these free and individualistic societies going to come from and what is the role of political leadership in all this?

A That's a very difficult question for me to answer.

Q Is the premise right?

A Yes, I would agree with your premise, though I don't know if it's a long-term trend or just a question of a generation or two. I think that societies will always be composed of people who are inner-directed and other-directed, to use the phrase from *The Lonely Crowd*. I think we will always be living in times where we will need people who seek their moral values within themselves and those who will need it from a kind of collective endorsement of certain beliefs. In other words, you will always have criminal processes, criminal codes, criminal laws which are based on views of the collectivity and you will always have individuals who have their own morals. To talk in the same terms as Thomas Aquinas, you will always have people who have morals of serfs, and you'll have some who have morals of princes. In other words, the morals of those whose conduct is based on orders, whether it be from God or from the church or from the father of the family or from the police in the state, and those whose conduct is not the result of having received an order but because they themselves have their own philosophy of the world, and their view of what is right and wrong is not based on external command but on internal belief. And I don't think that will change as long as men exist and societies exist.

What I was indicating I believe at the very outset of this meeting, though, was that sociological pressures will at some period set up stronger states and therefore have a more mono-lithic approach to morals, and individuals in that society will have to sort of either believe or write or think in secret. And you will have other periods when, in the kind of myth that Jean-Jacques Rousseau believed in, we will all freely obey the laws because we love the freedom and we love the results of the collective will.

So, as I indicated earlier, I think we obviously have been going through in your society and ours in very recent years a period where there is no slave morality, at least consciously; there is just the morality of what you call individuality: I will do my thing. And whether it's right or wrong by the laws of the state or by the church that my parents belong to is irrele-vant: I will do my thing; I will set up my own morality.

What I am merely trying to say is that is not a stable posi-tion for everyone in a society to be in. The very existence of a society needs a certain number of consensuses to exist, and you can still agree to them freely as princes, to use Aquinas' term. But there has to be that kind of consensus; otherwise you have a disorder, you have anarchy, you have the terror of the French revolution, and then you have the counter-swing to authoritarianism which as I was saying is what is perhaps threatening us now. And you see this even in the way the hip-pie movement has changed in the past few years. Having started out as expressions of individuality and freedom, it was becoming cliquish and extraordinarily tribal. The movement became a return to tribalism as soon as it became a collective phenomenon. They were looking for reassurance not in the church or in the family but in the peer group and they were no longer living – though they thought they were – a morality of free men but of slaves. They were slaves to that particular de-ity.

Interview with James Reston, New York Times
21 December 1971

The law of justice contained in the Torah and in the Talmudic traditions would not in itself have been adequate to provide a source of unity for the Jews. Their desire to embody God's word would not have been satisfied by individual obedience, nor by conformity reserved for an élite. Their instinct for achievement, their pragmatic inclinations, their need to rally, seem to have required more than the abstract ideal of a code. This is so for men everywhere: what man holds to be true, what he believes, must become the framework and the fibre of his existence.

But this characteristic is unusually strong among the Jewish people, as has been demonstrated by their two major institutions: the family and the synagogue. Although the concept of the family in one form or another is almost universal, it is for the Jews more solidly and undeniably based on the exchange of love between a man and a woman. Flesh of my flesh, bone of my bone! Wondrous Jewish words which literally breathed life into the concept of the couple. To this day, the entire Western world has modelled its family on the Jewish family. Where else would the gentiles have learned so well the lessons of conjugal and parental justice? What other family respects so highly its continuity and the integrity of each of its members, as shown by the practice of the Kadish? As for the synagogue, it is still the prototype of assembly, its rules protecting the right of all to knowledge, whether rich or poor, scholar or humble beginner ...

We know of many kinds of prejudice but there is a particular persistence to anti-semitism. Some people, carrying from generation to generation a deeply rooted malevolence, still cannot forgive Israel its distinctiveness, the three-fold gift of transcendence, individual worth and justice. To walk in God's ways, to love one's fellow man, and to be just in one's dealings, what unforgivable madness! And yet, I say, for any man worthy of the name, it is anti-semitism that is unforgivable.

The people of Canada condemn any defamation based on race or religion. As the Chairman has said, the government has introduced a bill in Parliament that will make the dissemination of hate literature a criminal offence. We took this step with determination though not without regret that it should be necessary in our country. Let this law be one more step towards the kind of society we want to build.

As the Jewish people know, the city of the just cannot be built overnight. And, as we all know, whoever seeks justice must be ready to risk everything for it.

I am aware that we are passing through a troubled period in this province and that being a member of a minority in these circumstances can be a cause for apprehension. I know that many members of the Jewish community share this feeling and have doubts about their future in Quebec. If I can speak as a member of one minority to another, Stick with it! Stick with it! With all your energies and abilities, play your full part in this society which you have helped to build and insist on your rights as members of it.

Family of Man Award Banquet of the Anti-Defamation League of B'nai B'rith, Montreal, 8 February 1970

Society cannot deny the necessity for new remedies, or for the creation of new rights adequate to the needs of the individual in the urban, technological society of today. Governments, courts, citizens, should all be prepared to admit that the underlying cause of most disorder is injustice ...

It was Paul Claudel who said in *Conversations dans le Loir-et-Cher*: 'Justice is never as beautiful as in disguise, when she wears not a bandage but a mask, and no one knows who she is'. Justice to me is a warm spirit, born of tolerance and wisdom, present everywhere, ready to serve the highest purposes of rational man.

To seek to create the just society must be amongst the highest of those human purposes. Because we are mortal and imperfect, it is a task we will never finish; no government or society ever will. But from our honest and ceaseless effort, we will draw strength and inspiration, we will discover new and better values, we will achieve an unprecedented level of human consciousness. On the never-ending road to perfect justice we will, in other words, succeed in creating the most humane and compassionate society possible.

National Conference on the Law, Ottawa, 1 February 1972

The Challenge of
Democracy

Democracy

We are in a beautiful garden. About us are handsome government buildings, imaginatively designed. Behind me is an important monument. These things are evidence of the goodness of life in Canada; of our ability to combine human and physical resources to make our land rich and productive; of our talent to govern ourselves by democratic processes; of our recollection of the harshness of the frontier and its occasional injustice; of our determination to make a better life for ourselves and our children.

Yet this very setting, this very tranquillity, this sense of orderliness and propriety makes me think how difficult it is for any of us to understand Louis Riel. What forces motivated this man? What social conditions led him to believe that nothing short of rebellion would serve the cause to which he had pledged himself? How many other Riels exist in Canada, beyond the fringe of accepted conduct, driven to believe that this country offers no answer to their needs and no solutions to their problems?

How many of us understand the loneliness, the sense of futility of such a man? How many of us are willing to concede that future historians, in chronicling the events of our lives, may choose to emphasize and applaud the activities, not of the privileged majority but of some little known leader of an unpopular minority?

On the South Nahanni River, NWT, August 1970

For me this is the lesson of Louis Riel. For me this is the reason why we are here ...

A democratic society and system of government, while among the grandest of human concepts, are among the most difficult to implement. In a democracy it is all too easy for the majority to forget the rights of the minority, and for a remote and powerful government to ignore its protests. It is all too easy, should disturbances erupt, to crush them in the name of law and order. We must never forget that, in the long run, a democracy is judged by the way the majority treats the minority. Louis Riel's battle is not yet won.

That is why I suggest that we should never respond to demands for just treatment by pointing to other examples of injustice. If a certain right is attacked or denied in one province, it is not a valid reason for refusing similar rights in another. Yet such excuses are offered; and this leads to a vicious circle in which no improvement in human liberties is possible. The rights of individual Canadians are too important to be used as bargaining counters. Every government must accept responsibility for the rights of the citizens within its own jurisdiction. Canada as a whole suffers when any of her citizens is denied his rights; for that injustice places the rights of all of us in jeopardy.

Unveiling of Louis Riel Monument, Regina, 2 October 1968

Q You have introduced quite a new technique in reaching people that has not been done by any of your predecessors and by very few leaders of other countries. That is, you get out and mix with students and you talk to them freely. Do you feel you do this as the Prime Minister or as a man who would like to get a certain point or message across?

A Much more the latter. Basically, I do that because I like to exchange ideas. I like to teach but I like to be taught. I like to learn things. I like to know what people think. I like them to know what I think. I especially believe – and this is, when you talk of students, what I especially want people to understand – that there is no great authority called the Prime Minister who gets messages from God, you know – who makes great laws.

Nor do I go around my office with a listening device, trying to take orders from Washington or Moscow or Rome or anything like that. The ideas that we come up with are basically the ideas of men who yesterday were merchants or lawyers or teachers and today happen to be the ministers of this government. That's essentially what I would like young people to understand, that perhaps our answers are not right as regards Vietnam or Biafra or NATO or the Indians. Perhaps they're not right, but we are not evil men trying to force a diabolical solution upon them. We are men who are coming up with answers as best we can and if they have better answers I'd like to know what they are. It's only in discussing with them that you can make them realize that many of their simplistic answers are just that, that they haven't really asked themselves all the difficult questions. And I find that if we come up with more ideas, it will only be accepted if the people are prepared for them, which means involving them, discussing with them, convincing them.

Interview with Jay Walz, New York Times, *22 November 1968*

It is a constant hazard of democracy that the loudest and most determined group is often that which holds the most extreme and reactionary views. We shall certainly hear from those who do not understand, or who are afraid of change. What we need is to rally the vast majority of reasonable and moderate Canadians, of both languages and all parties, who believe in an improved and more equitable federalism.

University of Moncton, Moncton, NB, 18 May 1969

Mr Speaker, I ask these persons who make bombs, who deny the peaceful exchange of ideas, who are unwilling to accept the decisions of authorized arbitrators, if these are the results they seek? If they consciously desire society to descend this spiral to destruction?

We in this House, as representatives of political parties, bear a heavy responsibility in these respects, Mr Speaker. We must not relinquish the burden which rests on our parties to offer to all Canadians acceptable vehicles for their political activities. If we do not provide proof of the vitality of the democratic process, we shall have failed our responsibilities and proved to the critics that the system is indeed at fault.

I wish to say on behalf of the Liberal Party, Mr Speaker, that we accept that challenge; that we intend, in the future as in the past, to be the voice of change; that we shall not forsake our role as advocate of the great mainstream of Canadians; that we intend to listen, to understand, to respond, to lead.
House of Commons, 24 October 1969

Q   A moment ago you said you like to use student energy in some way. In this country just a week ago we had a moratorium which the government said they would refuse to take any notice of. How specifically could student energy be used by government? How are you going to go about using it?

A   Well, I was giving two examples a moment ago. I think by lowering the voting age you can give students and young people generally a greater participation in the decision-making processes; and I believe that in the consultative process they can be involved much more if either they form their own political movements or they join existing ones. I am talking now of participation in the political sphere. I think this is the essence of your question. If you talk of moratoriums I think it is very important for governments to listen, to take notice of the feelings of the very important segment of the population. But there is a distinction between consultation and participation and decision-making. I think that in our democratic governments, which are essentially representative governments, parliamentary ones, I think the decision must always be taken by the representatives of the people. I am not a believer that foreign policy can be made in the streets or that policy of any kind should be determined by masses or mobs, whether they be of students or other groups. We all know the theory of the right to revolt, but when society provides – especially as it does today – enough affluence that people cannot claim lack of education, they can't claim lack of accessibility to the sources of knowledge, if they are students I do not think there is, by and large, an excuse to resort to violence. I think that we have access to peaceful means of change. They are sometimes difficult and sometimes too slow for the impatience of youth. They think that elections come only too seldom. But you know I have the strongest disapproval for people who think that by pressure, by making enough noise or raising enough signs, they can make the decisions. I think they should influence the decisions. I think their input should be received. But I think they are wrong when they say, 'Well, the government has not listened to us because it has not done what everyone wants it to do'. It has to, on balance, make what it believes is the best choice and then it's up to the citizens including young people to throw it out if the choices are not satisfactory.

'Teach-In', Australian National University, Canberra, Australia
18 May 1970

It is a matter of deep regret and grave concern to me, as I am sure it is to all honourable members, that the condition of our country makes necessary this proclamation [of the War Measures Act]. We in this House have all felt very strongly, I know, that democracy was nowhere in a healthier state than in Canada; that nowhere was there less need for frustrated men to turn to violence to attain their political ends. I still believe firmly that this is so. Yet in recent years we have been forced to acknowledge the existence within Canada of a new and terrifying type of person – one who in earlier times would have been described as an anarchist, but who is now known as a violent revolutionary. These persons allege that they are seeking social change through novel means. In fact they are seeking the destruction of the social order through clandestine and violent means.

Faced with such persons, and confronted with authoritative assessments of the seriousness of the risk to persons and property in the Montreal area, the government had no responsible choice but to act as it did last night. Given the rapid deterioration of the situation as mentioned by Prime Minister Bourassa, and given the expiration of the time offered for the release of the hostages, it became obvious that the urgency of the situation demanded rapid action. The absence both of adequate time to take other steps or of alternative legislative authority dictated the use of the War Measures Act. After informing the leaders of the opposition parties of our intention to act in this fashion, and following receipt of the letters that I tabled a moment ago, the government proclaimed the Act.

The government recognizes that the authority contained in the Act is much broader than is required in the present situation, notwithstanding the seriousness of the events. For that reason the regulations which were adopted permit the exercise of only a limited number of the powers available under the Act. Nevertheless, I wish to make it clear today that the government regards the use of the War Measures Act as only an interim and, in the sense mentioned above, somewhat unsatisfactory measure.

Following the passage of enough time to give the government the necessary experience to assess the type of statute which may be required in these circumstances, it is my firm intention to discuss with the leaders of the opposition parties the desirability of introducing legislation of a less comprehensive nature. In this respect I earnestly solicit from the leaders and from all honourable members constructive suggestions for the amendment of the regulations. Such suggestions will be given careful consideration for possible inclusion in any new statute.

May I say in conclusion, Mr Speaker, that no Canadian takes less lightly than I the seriousness of the present situation in Canada and the gravity of the measures which the government has been asked to assume in order to meet that situation. Coincidentally, the fate of the two kidnapped hostages weighs very heavily in my mind, as it does on all of us ...

To those who will voice concern at the extent of the powers assumed by the government under this procedure, I can only say that I sympathize with their attitude, and applaud them for speaking out. I hasten to suggest, however, that the legislative record of this Parliament in the field of individual liberties contributes unequivocally to its credibility and good faith.

I promise that the House shall be kept fully informed if any changes in the regulations are made. Furthermore, I pledge that all extraordinary powers will be withdrawn as soon as it has been demonstrated that there is a cessation of the violence and the threats of violence which made necessary their introduction. I intend to repeat that assurance and offer an explanation of government activities in this matter to the Canadian people through the public media later today.

Before I sit down, Mr Speaker, it would be inappropriate were I not to mention to the House my gratitude for the understanding which has been offered me in the last 24 hours by the leaders of the opposition parties and by certain members of the Privy Council, including the right honourable member for Prince Albert and the right honourable Lester B. Pearson. For their wise counsel I say, thank you.

House of Commons, 16 October 1970

I am speaking to you at a moment of grave crisis, when violent and fanatical men are attempting to destroy the unity and the freedom of Canada. One aspect of that crisis is the threat which has been made on the lives of two innocent men. These are matters of the utmost gravity and I want to tell you what the government is doing to deal with them.

What has taken place in Montreal in the past two weeks is not unprecedented. It has happened elsewhere in the world on several recent occasions; it could happen elsewhere within Canada. But Canadians have always assumed that it could not happen here and as a result we are doubly shocked that it has.

Our assumption may have been naive, but it was understandable; understandable because democracy flourishes in Canada; understandable because individual liberty is cherished in Canada.

Notwithstanding these conditions — partly because of them — it has now been demonstrated to us by a few misguided persons just how fragile a democratic society can be, if democracy is not prepared to defend itself, and just how vulnerable to blackmail are tolerant, compassionate people.

Because the kidnappings and the blackmail are most familiar to you, I shall deal with them first.

The governments of Canada and Quebec have been told by groups of self-styled revolutionaries that they intend to murder in cold blood two innocent men unless their demands are met. The kidnappers claim they act as they do in order to draw attention to instances of social injustice. But I ask them whose attention are they seeking to attract. The government of Canada? The government of Quebec? Every government in this country is well aware of the existence of deep and important social problems. And every government to the limit of its resources and ability is deeply committed to their solution. But not by kidnappings and bombings. By hard work. And if any doubt exists about the good faith or the ability of any government, there are opposition parties ready and willing to be given an opportunity to govern. In short, there is available everywhere in Canada an effective mechanism to change governments by peaceful means. It has been employed by disenchanted voters again and again.

Who are the kidnap victims? To the victims' families they are husbands and fathers. To the kidnappers their identity is immaterial. The kidnappers' purposes would be served equally well by having in their grip you or me, or perhaps some child. Their purpose is to exploit the normal, human feelings of Canadians and to bend those feelings of sympathy into instruments for their own violent and revolutionary ends.

What are the kidnappers demanding in return for the lives of these men? Several things. For one, they want their grievances aired by force in public on the assumption, no doubt, that all right-thinking persons would be persuaded that the problems of the world can be solved by shouting slogans and insults.

They want more, they want the police to offer up as a sacrificial lamb a person whom they assume assisted in the lawful arrest and proper conviction of certain of their criminal friends.

They also want money. Ransom money.

They want still more. They demand the release from prison of seventeen criminals, and the dropping of charges against six other men, all of whom they refer to as political prisoners. Who are these men who are held out as latter-day patriots and martyrs? Let me describe them to you.

Three are convicted murderers; five others were jailed for manslaughter; one is serving a life imprisonment after having pleaded guilty to numerous charges related to bombings; another has been convicted of seventeen armed robberies; two were once paroled but are now back in jail awaiting trial on charges of robberies.

Yet we are being asked to believe that these persons have been unjustly dealt with, that they have been imprisoned as a result of their political opinions, and that they deserve to be freed immediately, without recourse to due process of law.

The responsibility of deciding whether to release one or other of these criminals is that of the federal government. It is a responsibility that the government will discharge according to law. To bow to the pressures of these kidnappers who demand that the prisoners be released would be not only an abdication of responsibility; it would lead to an increase in terrorist activities in Quebec. It would be as well an invitation to terrorism and kidnapping across the country. We might well find ourselves facing an endless series of demands for the release of criminals from jails, from coast to coast, and we would find that the hostages could be innocent members of your family or mine.

At the moment the FLQ is holding hostage two men in the Montreal area, one a British diplomat, the other a Quebec cabinet minister. They are threatened with murder. Should governments give in to this crude blackmail we would be facing the breakdown of the legal system, and its replacement by the law of the jungle. The government's decision to prevent this from happening is not taken just to defend an important principle; it is taken to protect the lives of Canadians from dangers of the sort I have mentioned. Freedom and personal security are safeguarded by laws; those laws must be respected in order to be effective.

If it is the responsibility of government to deny the demands of the kidnappers, the safety of the hostages is without question the responsibility of the kidnappers. Only the most twisted form of logic could conclude otherwise. Nothing that either the government of Canada or the government of Quebec has done or failed to do, now or in the future, could possibly excuse any injury to either of these two innocent men. The guns pointed at their heads have FLQ fingers on the triggers. Should any injury result, there is no explanation that could condone the acts. Should there be harm done to these men, the government promises unceasing pursuit of those responsible.

During the past twelve days, the governments of Canada and Quebec have been engaged in constant consultations. The course followed in this matter had the full support of both governments, and of the Montreal municipal authorities. In order to save the lives of Mr Cross and Mr Laporte, we have engaged in communications with the kidnappers.

The offer of the federal government to the kidnappers of safe conduct out of Canada to a country of their choice, in return for the delivery of the hostages, has not yet been taken up; neither has the offer of the government of Quebec to recommend parole for the five prisoners eligible for parole.

This offer of safe conduct was made only because Mr Cross and Mr Laporte might be able to identify their kidnappers and to assist in their prosecution; by offering the kidnappers safe exit from Canada we removed from them any possible motivation for murdering their hostages.

Let me turn now to the broader implications of the threat represented by the FLQ and similar organizations.

If a democratic society is to continue to exist, it must be able to root out the cancer of an armed, revolutionary movement that is bent on destroying the very basis of our freedom. For that reason the government, following an analysis of the facts, including requests of the government of Quebec and the City of Montreal for urgent action, decided to proclaim the War Measures Act. It did so at 4.00 this morning, in order to permit the full weight of government to be brought quickly to bear on all those persons advocating or practising violence as a means of achieving political ends.

The War Measures Act gives sweeping powers to the government. It also suspends the operation of the Canadian Bill of Rights. I can assure you that the government is most reluctant to seek such powers, and did so only when it became crystal clear that the situation could not be controlled unless some extraordinary assistance was made available on an urgent basis.

The authority contained in the Act will permit governments to deal effectively with the nebulous yet dangerous challenge to society represented by the terrorist organizations. The criminal law as it stands is simply not adequate to deal with systematic terrorism.

The police have therefore been given certain extraordinary

powers necessary for the effective detection and elimination of conspiratorial organizations which advocate the use of violence. These organizations, and membership in them, have been declared illegal. The powers include the right to search and arrest without warrant, to detain suspected persons without the necessity of laying specific charges immediately, and to detain persons without bail.

These are strong powers and I find them as distasteful as I am sure do you. They are necessary, however, to permit the police to deal with persons who advocate or promote the violent overthrow of our democratic system. In short, I assure you that the government recognizes its grave responsibilities in interfering in certain cases with civil liberties, and that it remains answerable to the people of Canada for its actions. The government will revoke this proclamation as soon as possible.

As I said in the House of Commons this morning, the government will allow sufficient time to pass to give it the necessary experience to assess the type of statute which may be required in the present circumstances.

It is my firm intention to discuss then with the leaders of the opposition parties the desirability of introducing legislation of a less comprehensive nature. In this respect, I earnestly solicit from the leaders and from all honourable members constructive suggestions for the amendment of the regulations. Such suggestions will be given careful consideration for possible inclusion in any new statute.

I recognize, as I hope do others, that this extreme position into which governments have been forced is in some respects a trap. It is a well-known technique of revolutionary groups who attempt to destroy society by unjustified violence to goad the authorities into inflexible attitudes. The revolutionaries then employ this evidence of alleged authoritarianism as justification for the need to use violence in their renewed attacks on the social structure. I appeal to all Canadians not to become so obsessed by what the government has done today in response to terrorism that they forget the opening play in this vicious game. That play was taken by the revolutionaries; they chose to use bombing, murder and kidnapping.

The threat posed by the FLQ terrorists and their supporters

is out of all proportion to their numbers. This follows from the fact that they act stealthily and because they are known to have in their possession a considerable amount of dynamite. To guard against the very real possibility of bombings directed at public buildings or utilities in the immediate future, the government of Quebec has requested the assistance of the Canadian Armed Forces to support the police in several places in the Province of Quebec. These forces took up their positions yesterday.

Violence, unhappily, is no stranger to this decade. The Speech from the Throne opening the current session of Parliament a few days ago said that 'we live in a period of tenseness and unease.' We must not overlook the fact, moreover, that violence is often a symptom of deep social unrest. This government has pledged that it will introduce legislation which deals not just with symptoms but with the social causes which often underlie or serve as an excuse for crime and disorder.

It was in that context that I stated in the House of Commons a year ago that there was no need anywhere in Canada for misguided or misinformed zealots to resort to acts of violence in the belief that only in this fashion could they accomplish change. There may be some places in the world where the law is so inflexible and so insensitive as to prompt such beliefs. But Canada is not such a place. I said then, and I repeat now, that those who would defy the law and ignore the opportunities available to them to right their wrongs and satisfy their claims will receive no hearing from this government.

We shall ensure that the laws passed by Parliament are worthy of respect. We shall also ensure that those laws are respected.

We have seen in many parts of Canada all too much evidence of violence in the name of revolution in the past twelve months. We are now able to see some of the consequences of violence. Persons who invoke violence are raising deliberately the level of hate in Canada. They do so at a time when the country must eliminate hate, and must exhibit tolerance and compassion in order to create the kind of society which we all desire. Yet those who disrespect legal processes create a danger that law-abiding elements of the community, out of anger and out of fear, will harden their attitudes and refuse to accommodate any change or remedy any shortcomings. They refuse because fear deprives persons of their normal sense of compassion and their normal sense of justice.

This government is not acting out of fear. It is acting to prevent fear from spreading. It is acting to maintain the rule of law without which freedom is impossible. It is acting to make clear to kidnappers and revolutionaries and assassins that in this country laws are made and changed by the elected representatives of all Canadians – not by a handful of self-selected dictators. Those who gain power through terror, rule through terror. The government is acting, therefore, to protect your life and your liberty.

The government is acting as well to ensure the safe return of Mr James Cross and Mr Pierre Laporte. I speak for millions of Canadians when I say to their courageous wives and families how much we sympathize with them for the nightmare to which they have been subjected, and how much we all hope and pray that it will soon conclude.

Canada remains one of the most wholesome and humane lands on this earth. If we stand firm, this current situation will soon pass. We will be able to say proudly, as we have for decades, that within Canada there is ample room for opposition and dissent, but none for intimidation and terror.

There are very few times in the history of any country when all persons must take a stand on critical issues. This is one of those times; this is one of those issues. I am confident that those persons who unleashed this tragic sequence of events with the aim of destroying our society and dividing our country will find that the opposite will occur. The result of their acts will be a stronger society in a unified country. Those who would have divided us will have united us.

I sense the unease which grips many Canadians today. Some of you are upset, and this is understandable. I want to reassure you that the authorities have the situation well in hand. Everything that needs to be done is being done; every level of government in this country is well prepared to act in your interests.

National television broadcast, 16 October 1970.

There are few occasions when the entire population of a country shares a single emotion, and senses a deep unity in the face of events. This is one of those occasions.

Canadians have witnessed in the past two weeks a series of events which was conceived in treachery and has been executed with cowardice. We have watched in horror as a small band of twisted men set in motion events designed to turn Canadian against Canadian. Their scheme has been a deliberate provocation of hate.

The men responsible for these crimes are not representative Canadians. They are members of a hard core devoted to a single purpose – to inspire within all of us fear and hatred and in this atmosphere to destroy our nation. They are beneath contempt.

In this moment of shock and grief, I know that all Canadians are deeply conscious of the benefits that flow from a tolerant, compassionate, and free society. We recognize that if we permit hatred and violence to grow and spread, these benefits will disappear.

We recognize that Pierre Laporte was a man who had devoted his life to the betterment of the people of Quebec. His adult life was dedicated to the attainment of social justice, of economic benefits and of individual liberties for his fellow citizens. His record of struggle and accomplishment sounds out like a trumpet in comparison to the whines of self-pity and the screams of hatred which have poured forth from the FLQ. Yet this was the man the FLQ murdered in cold blood.

We must expect that these vicious men may attempt again to shake our will in the days ahead. I speak for all of you when I say that any such attempt shall fail.

Canada grieves for Madame Laporte and her children. On your behalf, I offer them deepest sympathy. They will know that the name of Pierre Laporte will be repeated by school children for generations as a symbol of steadfast opposition to division, disunity and hatred in Canada. Those who recognize the need for change in Canadian society will be reassured in their quest by the knowledge that in this land there are many men who share the dedication of Pierre Laporte, a mere few who follow the FLQ.

Those responsible for this crime will be found and will be

dealt with in the calm and dispassionate atmosphere of Canadian courts. The FLQ has sown the seeds of its own destruction. It has revealed that it has no mandate but terror, no policies but violence, and no solutions but murder. Savagery is alien to Canadians; it always will be, for collectively we will not tolerate it.

National television broadcast, 18 October 1970

Mr Speaker, the House learned late Saturday night of the brutal, cowardly slaying of Pierre Laporte. That tragic event is evidence of the moral wasteland occupied by the FLQ. Their activities these past few days have been designed to turn Canadian against Canadian. The FLQ scheme has been a deliberate provocation of hate. Their purpose is to inspire within all of us fear and hatred, and in this atmosphere to destroy our nation.

They will not succeed.

Canadians for too long have known freedom, practised tolerance, and enjoyed the benefits of our rich cultural diversity. They will not be tricked by such a transparent device; they will not be dominated by criminals. Canadians have seen, too, the bitter and divisive effects in other countries when hatred is met by hate, when crime is followed by vengeance, when reason is overcome totally by emotion.

Made up of men full of hatred, the FLQ resorts to violence to inspire hate, feed it and to spread it insidiously, hoping that disorder, confusion and panic will then prevail.

Such is its first purpose. Such is the trap it is setting for us: to turn Canadians against Canadians, to divide us through hatred and racism, to aggravate disagreements between generations even to the point where they can no longer be reconciled. But those fanatics are perhaps even more diabolic in their need to inspire hatred for themselves – blind hatred. Thus they could bring us down to their level and degrade our society.

Pierre Laporte devoted his life to the betterment of the people of Quebec. Honourable members will have an opportunity tomorrow to pay their respects to this man. In the interim, all Canada grieves for Mme Laporte and her children ...

This deed will not deter progress toward needed social change; rather, it will inspire the many persons in all parts of Canada who share the broad vision of Pierre Laporte.

By this deed the FLQ has sown the seeds of its own destruction. It has revealed that it has no mandate but terror, no policies but violence, and no solutions but murder. It is alien to all that is Canadian. It will not survive.

Those men with hatred in their hearts thought they could divide us in tragedy; instead they bring us together.

For the only passion which must drive us now is the passion for justice. Through justice, we will get rid of the perversion of terrorism. Through justice, we will find peace and freedom.

House of Commons, 19 October 1970

A properly functioning democracy looks forward as well as back; it offers citizens a creative as well as a monitoring role; it is a partnership between people and Parliament.

You are here as part of such a system. Here, at this conference, you have an opportunity to view future need against past performance and to produce policies for government action. In this conference you will be given an accounting by your elected representatives of the extent to which they have abided by your past policy recommendations, and you will be given an opportunity to express your confidence – or lack of it – in the leadership of the Liberal Party.

These are important tasks – important for the Liberal Party, important for Canada. And, in the particular climate of this decade, important for democracy. Your presence here is proof that democracy is able to take stock of its shortcomings, and able to work to remedy them. This kind of conference is the answer to those persons who would have us believe that policies can be influenced only by coercion, that an accounting can be obtained only by violence, and that leadership can be changed only by assassination.

For some years we have witnessed with concern the activities elsewhere of persons who preach these policies of hate. This autumn we watched with horror as they erupted in Canada. The government moved to counter this threat to our democratic structure, but as it did so it was forced to divert its attention from the tasks which had been occupying it; the tasks which need to be attended to in order to create in Canada a land which offers to all Canadians economic benefit, social justice and an enhanced quality of life.

We heard these hysterical persons voice their concern about the economy, about the underprivileged, and about the casualties of our society; concerns shared by us all. Yet the acts of violence which they brought upon us contributed in no way to an easing of those problems. Quite the opposite. The violence and the terrorism forced governments to transfer resources and energies from the very programmes designed to assist the economically handicapped areas of Canada. Legislation of the kind that Parliament was forced to consider went not one inch towards solving the problems of the unemployed, or alleviating the plight of the urban slum dweller, or providing better social conditions for the people of Canada.

Acts of terrorism, if multiplied several fold, could force the social and democratic institutions of this country into a totally defensive posture. But that will not happen. It will not happen because this government will not permit it, because Parliament will not permit it, because Canadians will not permit it.

Both liberty and democracy, in order to exist, require the other. Neither can survive, moreover, without some ability to defend themselves against those who would destroy them. The threat is not always, indeed it is seldom, from external sources. It comes on one occasion from the criminal, on another from the wealthy; at one time it will be the intransigence of the bureaucracy, on another the cleverness of politicians. Democracy and liberty must face sometimes the hysteria of a mob and at other times the calculated plans of a handful of conspirators. They are constantly under the attack of the bigoted and stupid; on occasion they need protection from the over-righteous and the super-patriotic. If anything be certain, it is that the continued vitality of neither liberty nor democracy can be assumed.

Canadians have lived in a land as free from restrictions as any, and far more than most. Our laws have reflected the extraordinary degree of tolerance, of give and take, which characterize the relationships amongst us. We are not burdened with loyalty oaths at universities or by police registrations at hotels. No one doubts in Canada that both police and military are firmly under the direction of elected political leaders. We

At the Carnaval Souvenir, Chicoutimi, February 1970

have not needed more stringent precautions; indeed we have flourished in their absence. Until the tragic events of recent weeks, political assassination had been unknown in Canada for more than a century. Violent opposition to the structure of government had broken out on occasion but had as its aim the reform of the system, or an improvement in its operation, not its destruction. Little wonder, therefore, that we all, collectively and individually, recoiled with horror at this new type of threat to our social and political order. Little wonder at the unease we all experienced at the introduction of stringent measures to contain the threat.

What we have found in these recent weeks of shock and self-examination is not that Canada has changed, not that life will never again be the same, but that in our previous dedication to common sense and reasonableness we have paid insufficient heed to the arrival in our midst of fanatics and barbarians. Persons of this sort are not reformers, for they have no alternatives to government programmes. They are not revolutionaries, for they propose no new structure of government. They are anarchists. They are willing to abandon every achievement of civilization, to forgo every hard-won accomplishment of men through the centuries. And in place of these achievements and accomplishments, they offer nothing.

Democracy need have no fear from open confrontation, for it is strengthened by the exposure of its weaknesses. Democracy does require, however, an atmosphere of honesty in order to flourish. Honesty, in turn, presupposes freedom of choice, not an absence of choice as a result of terror. To those who would substitute something else for democracy, who prefer totalitarianism – of the right or of the left – to freedom, I joyfully challenge them to political battle.

But there is nothing honest and nothing free about coercion and blackmail. In the result, neither example nor precept is adequate to counter them. More is needed. A democracy evidences its weakness, not its strength, if it stands passive and views with disdain undemocratic activities aimed at its destruction. When challenged last month by terrorists, the government did not permit indecision, or its distaste for the task, to stand in its way. It accepted its responsibility and it acted in the way which is now familiar to all of you.

We must, of course, remain vigilant and on guard – but the

crisis is now in hand. The government is able now gradually to turn its energies back to the problems which require undivided attention in order that Canada will be a better place for Canadians. For its part the Liberal Party is able to face its own ideal, to re-examine its own tenets and policies, and pronounce its views on the direction which it proposes this country should take.

Liberal Policy Conference, Ottawa, 20 November 1970

Whatever our political ideology, whatever our economic or social system, whatever our geographic location, the phenomenon which is common to all of us is change. I have not the slightest doubt that the decade which has just begun will be witness to more changes in most spheres of human activity than has any other decade in history. Changes of this order bring with them problems, and in most instances they are problems for governments.

Democracies offer every facility for change. Political and judicial processes are, or should be, geared for change. Yet in this turbulent age in which we live, nation after nation is learning that these processes are too slow, that the rate of actual change outpaces by far the rate of expected change. In that event, as in an electrical system designed in an older, less demanding time, the pressure of the new load becomes so intense that fuses blow and the apparatus breaks down. All too often the flash point is accompanied by violence. Violence is no stranger to this decade, Madame Prime Minister, either in my country as we have learned to our sorrow in recent weeks, or in yours from which has come the important lesson that *ahimsa*, non-violence, is not weakness. In dealing with violence, governments must be firm, but never should they fall into the trap of the extremists and – through extended reliance upon counter-violence inflame still further the activities of the dissidents. The lesson given us by India is the lesson of attempting to understand, of probing beyond the symptoms, of seeking out the root causes of dissatisfaction, and of administering to the basic illness.

Prime Minister Gandhi's luncheon, New Delhi, India 12 January 1971

Not all things have changed in the past century ... One constant, unquestionably, is the critical importance of Canada's manufacturing industries to our capacity to meet our economic and social objectives over the years ahead. Today, these industries contribute more than one-quarter of Canada's real domestic product, account for better than one in every five Canadian jobs, and represent a major investment in the future of this country. That contribution is extemely important, and will be no less important in years to come. The fulfilment of the promise of Canada will depend not so much upon the specific challenges of today as it will depend upon the way in which our society – including our manufacturing industries – develops its responses to these challenges, and to the challenges of tomorrow and the day after.
Canadian Manufacturers' Association, Toronto, 8 June 1971

Today is the 104th occasion on which Canadians have paused to reflect on their past, assess their present and conjecture about their future. Conditions have varied considerably during the many years since Confederation, and the mood of Canada has varied with them. There have been periods of peace and of war, others of economic depression and of expansive prosperity, still others both of doubt and of confidence.

Seldom, however, in that century and a fraction have events been so subject to sudden alteration, and conditions in the world so uncertain, as they are today. Mankind is passing through an era of major change, perhaps the most intensive in recorded history; an era more significant than that of the industrial revolution, one of more daring accomplishment than the renaissance. Those of us alive in the 1970s are both observers and participants in a decade of adventure and excitement. It is not the easiest period in history; it is not for the complacent or the self-satisfied. It is marked by instability and confusion. But these are the marks of every great age, and who would prefer to live at any other time?

Canadians are well equipped by nature and experience to contribute to such an age, and to profit from it. Our history has not permitted us to relax in contentment, our climate has been a constant challenge, our population has never been monolithic in origin, and seldom have we taken ourselves too seriously. We are identifiable because of our moderation and our affability, our tolerance of others and our acceptance of change. We believe that our social institutions are of our choosing and for our benefit; we prefer, in this country, to lead lives in which courtesy and good humour and common sense are still regarded as desirable attributes.

Canadians have much for which to be grateful and much about which to be excited. It is well, on this July 1st, to look at the world about us and at Canada's good fortune.

Message to the Nation, 1 July 1971

Q The churches which identify with the dispossessed and the repressed in certain parts of the world – South Africa, Rhodesia, Mozambique, even to an extent in the Middle East – are finding that by their identification and by their assistance, that they are actually supporting groups that have turned to violence in order to end the violence under which they have lived. The World Council of Churches, for example, is in trouble over giving grants of money for medical supplies and so on to such groups. I have read recently some of the things you've said about violence and the tremendous question it raises in our time. Are you completely non-violent? Or do you think there's a case for a suppressed people trying to end their repression by resorting to violence?

A In my political philosophy, I think that there sometimes is room for violence. In my religion I really cannot think of cases where violence is justified. I know the usual answer of Christ using violence to get the sellers out of the temple, but to me this was impatience rather than violence.

Q Personally, you're almost pacifist?

A No. I think that religions must seek peace and love and therefore be pacifist. But, here again, when the religious principles, like the philosophical, are translated into reality, sometimes the reality forces violence on you, and there is no escape from it, and then I don't think it's something you should try to hide your face from.

Q If you were a young American of draft age called up to go to Viet Nam, would you come to Canada?

A I couldn't say because I – you know, this type of hypothetical situation – God knows what I would think if I were of that age. But I could perhaps answer your question indirectly by saying that those who make the conscientious judgment that they must not participate in this war and who become draft-dodgers, have my complete sympathy, and indeed our political approach has been to give them access to Canada whether they are draft-dodgers, or even more serious, deserters from the ranks of their armed forces. That, perhaps, could enlighten you at least on my theoretical approach. I see nothing wrong with it. I think that the only ultimate guide we have is our conscience, and if the law of the land goes against our conscience I think we should disobey the law. But because I also am a deep believer in the civil society, I think we should be prepared to pay the consequences of breaking the law and that is either paying the penalty for it, or leaving the country. I feel perhaps I didn't deal with the question of violence in depth. If you want to return to it I won't object.

Q   Well, let's go back to this, because I have gathered you have said you're not judging those who, under specific circumstances, turn to violence.

A   That's right. It's the circumstances which one also has to have a philosophy about. Let's take a specific example. If you live in a society where those who govern society and determine its path do not respect freedom of speech and freedom of religion, freedom of choice, freedom of assembly, and if there is no democratic process and no way to change the order of things by reason and peace and love and so on, and if, as a result of that, certain ideas in which you believe are being crushed, then I think the only way you can defend yourself against this violence is in using violence of your own. I can see that in certain political situations you have to use force to overthrow police states, for instance. As a politician I've never had to face that because I've always lived in a democratic society. But I think violence is counter-productive and it is bad in democratic societies.

Q   Professor Joseph Hromadka said some years ago that he was more fearful of anti-Communism as it was being expressed in certain parts of the West than of Communism. Have you any comment on the policy of trying to contain Communism with military force in other countries?

A   Yes. I don't believe you can contain ideas by military
force. I believe military force can be used to redress or change
the balance of power in the world, but I think that that's always a losing operation if you're not trying to do it in a way
which corresponds to the basic desires of the people on whom
you are acting. Who is it that said that 'you have not conver-
ted a man because you have silenced him'? This is true of the
use of the military on people. As you gather from my earlier
answer, I am peaceful but I am not a pacifist in the philosophical sense. I recognize that in some cases it's more important
to have freedom and justice than to have peace. Sometimes
you must live in a violent world in order to get greater justice.
But I think all of us, politicians and churchmen, should do our
utmost to change the society so that there would be no need
for violence. This is the beauty of the democratic process: it
permits that subjective view of justice – which everyone holds
– permits that subjective view to express itself peacefully
through discussion, through reason and through the voting
process. I'm far from believing that we've solved the problem
of violence in the twentieth century and that's why I'm not
discouraged that we still have the Biafras and the Northern
Irelands and the East Pakistans and, for that matter, violence
in American or Canadian cities. I think that as the guardian
of justice elected by the people it's our duty to use whatever
forms of force – police, army – to make sure that at least the
freedom of choice is preserved. You know it is a false dichot-
omy between order and freedom. Not too long ago I was asked
which my preference would be. Obviously I prefer freedom, but I know, and I think all history has told us, that freedom cannot flow from anarchy and disorder. Freedom can
flow from order. That is not to say that freedom always flows
from order because you can have a totalitarian order and you
can have an undemocratic order from which freedom will not
flow, but the surest way to destroy freedom is to have chaos.
United Church Observer, September 1971

There is not, in my view, an irreconcilable conflict between
the individual and freedom on the one hand, and government
and authority on the other.

No society has ever regarded itself with such distaste that it did not provide for the protection of its own basic structure against acts of violence mounted outside the accepted channels of opposition. Nor does Canadian society today. This should alarm no one, for in Canada there are a variety of political safeguards – freedom of speech, freedom of assembly, free elections, to name a few. When these safeguards exist, it is irresponsible for anyone to suggest that violence is necessary to right political wrongs. It is equally irresponsible for anyone to justify, in the name of a cause or a principle, the use of violence against innocent individuals.

In Canada, we all have known the agony and the trauma of political violence. We have been exposed to the horror of bombing, kidnapping and political murder. I am referring to the activities of the FLQ and to the events of October 1970. During that awesome month, the government had a critical and delicate task – to measure the balance between the rights of the individual and the activities of public agencies. It also had to demonstrate to citizen and revolutionary alike that it was capable of governing, that it was not willing to be cowed by persons acting in concert and attempting to coerce society for their own aims. And the burden was greater. It was to protect innocents against the wholly immoral and merciless activities of self-styled patriots.

Those who contend that society is itself violent, and that the use of violence against it is justified, lack an essential ingredient in their argument. They speak as dissidents, as members of a minority possessing no mandate from the community whose restructuring they propose. They are a peculiar breed, possessed of a solitary arrogance. Incapable of employing the opportunities made available to them by society in order to bring about changes through persuasion, they rationalize the killing and maiming of innocent bystanders as evidence of devotion to their cause.

A democratic society is terribly exposed to this kind of intimidation. The more free it is, the more tolerant its peoples are to the advocacy of all forms of government, the more lenient its police are to individual variations of conduct, the more vulnerable it is to perfidy of this sort. And the more reluctant is government to respond in extraordinary fashion. But there can be no question of the duty that any government must discharge. It is the duty to act in such fashion that the social order remains able to protect the life of its members, to guarantee the right of dissent, and to prevent the forces of restraint from falling prey to the lure of reaction and authoritarianism – in short, to ensure the continuing possibility of change. It is an abdiction of responsibility for a government to be hospitable to anarchy. By so doing, it contributes to a climate of fear, encourages negative manifestations of the human instinct for survival, and invites tribalism and lawlessness. In that kind of environment there is no safety, no order, and no protection for the unpopular, for the minorities, or for the weak.

What I have sought for years, in my opposition to those who support violence, is some evidence amongst them of a radical intellectual dignity. Those who advocate violence as a means of attaining greater freedom within a democracy are suffering from a fearful misconception: that there is somehow a conflict between man's instincts for justice for his fellows and liberty for himself. Rational men and women know in their hearts and minds that this is not so. It is the task of government to demonstrate to militants of both right and left that there is no conflict, that justice and liberty must co-exist in a single community. But it is also the task of government to preserve for all citizens their freedoms – from assault, from fear, from illegal acts of all kinds. The authority of democratic governments to protect their citizens finds its legitimacy in the will of the people. Indeed, the use of force within the law to safeguard the rights and interests of each and every member of the body politic, is a prerogative of freely elected governments. It is a prerogative which, if abused in any way, undermines respect for authority and for law. Those who challenge these principles challenge the foundations of the open society.

National Conference on the Law, Ottawa, 1 February 1972

In the short run, a party could maintain itself in power by responding to each crisis as it arose. But if it concentrated only on immediate solutions, it would be ignoring the underlying conditions which caused each crisis. It would be prescribing for the symptoms rather than the disease. Eventually the crises would accumulate and overwhelm the party.

A party's principal concern should not be how to settle a particular strike – let the Minister of Labour and the Cabinet worry about that. It should be to resolve the continuing crisis in industrial relations by working out a better system of reconciling the interests of labour, management and the public. That task is not only more difficult, it is much more important.

In a matter as familiar and as obvious as water pollution, we are paying for the decisions taken, or avoided, ten years ago. At the end of the 70s we will be living with the results of decisions taken at the beginning of the decade. Planning, whether it is by a political party or a government or a private company, must operate in a scale of time which is sufficient to permit it to alter the future.

We are like the pilots of a supersonic airplane. By the time an airport comes into the pilot's field of vision, it is too late to begin the landing procedure. Such planes must be navigated by radar. A political party, in formulating policy, can act as a society's radar. The analogy, of course, is very incomplete. As members of a political party we should be thinking not only of the type of goals we wish to achieve in our society, but of their relative importance, and of the best means of achieving them within a reasonable time.

Liberal Party Conference, Harrison Hot Springs, BC, *21 November 1969*

Parliament

The role of the opposition is an important one and I do not wish here to embark on a judgment of their performance; I'd rather leave that to the Canadian electorate. I do think, however, that it is now more important than ever for the opposition to present realistic alternatives, especially on fundamental questions. I don't think that at this sophisticated stage in our democracy people conceive of the opposition as merely a tool with which to find scandals in the ranks of the government or to level criticism or jibes at specific actions. I think the opposition will more and more be called upon to suggest alternatives, which means spelling out their own policy rather than merely attacking ours.

The Canadian public is participating in the discussion of many of the major issues. Academics are participating; editorial writers, newspapers and the magazines are arguing for certain courses of action and, I think, more and more the opposition will also have to state its priorities and its solutions to specific problems.

A kind of game has been going on for a long while in the democracies where opposition parties criticize the government for raising taxes and at the same time call for vastly increasing expenditures in various fields. I think this kind of game is gone and done with, and it's a good thing.

Answers to Questions by Charles Templeton, Maclean's Magazine, *3 April 1969*

The landing this week of a man on the moon is vivid evidence of the speed of change in men's lives. In a time frame of less than seven decades in length, a period shorter than man's biblical life span, man has ceased to remain earthbound and has reached out into his universe with a skill and a success that promise future change at an even more bewildering rate of acceleration. If this Parliament, which is charged with the responsibility of assimilating these technological changes into legislation for the benefit of Canadians, cannot keep pace, then Canadians will seek other institutions which are capable of doing so. We have no choice. Parliament is not inviolate to rules of nature. It must be relevant. It will adapt or it will perish.

At this point in time, with social structures in greater ferment than on any occasion in history, with scientific achievements of fantastic magnitude, with concepts and applications of concepts so complex and revealing as to stagger and refute previous economic and demographic truths, at this time in history legislative institutions which fail to reform themselves do so at peril of their own destruction.

Here are some of the Parliamentary reforms which have been made this year.

First, we have participated fully, Mr Speaker, in implementing the wise proposal that the office which you fill with such distinction be separated totally from party politics.

We have in addition provided, for the first time in the history of this country, large sums of money to the opposition parties to permit them to employ their own research staffs and so be better able to fulfil effectively their proper function of examining and considering government legislation, of pointing out weaknesses and proposing, if necessary, alternatives. But this is not all. This government has been the first to provide to the opposition adequate and regular opportunities to bring into this House matters of debate of its own choice. The importance of this latter provision cannot be over-emphasized.

Hitherto, apart from supply motions which were generally concentrated in one or two short periods each session, the opposition has been able to control totally the topics discussed

Dominion Day celebrations on Parliament Hill, 1968

during debate on only two occasions: during the Throne Speech debate and during the debate following the presentation of the budget. In short, the opposition has had few opportunities in the past to choose the subject of debate.

For these reasons the rule changes introduced and passed by Parliament this year are outstanding achievements of which we are proud.

We are told that we are bent on muzzling the opposition, Mr Speaker, but from now on, under the reforms which we have proposed to the House, of approximately 160 or 170 sitting days in a reasonable parliamentary year, 8 days are to be occupied by the debate on the Address in reply to the Speech from the Throne, 6 by the Budget debate, and an additional 28 are earmarked for the business of Supply and are allocated as opposition days, to be distributed throughout the sitting year so as to permit the opposition at frequent and regular intervals to challenge government policy on points of its own choosing. This means that 42 days in each session – approximately 25 per cent of the session – are days controlled by the opposition.

I think it proper to observe, Mr Speaker, that in the current procedural debate, the opposition has chosen either not to mention at all, or to pass very lightly over, the introduction of this important parliamentary safeguard. Far from fettering Parliament, this government has moved further than any in the history of Canada to assure to the opposition regular and adequate opportunities to attack the government's record, and we have given them the means, Mr Speaker.

It is normal in any legislature that bills must often be given priority by the government, not because of their importance, but because of their urgency. What happens in Canada but not elsewhere is that if unreasonable debate delays passage of such urgent bills, then the important ones may never be dealt with at all. The result is that a form of closure is introduced not by government but by the opposition; closure of government business by exclusion of it from the Commons' order paper through the lack of time to deal properly with it; closure, Mr Speaker, by frustration.

Every democratic assembly requires some procedure for

turning discussion into decision. In the parliaments of the
United Kingdom, of Australia, of New Zealand, and of India,
there are procedures for bringing on decisions. It is simply
non-responsive to this need to say, as honourable members opposite interject from time to time, that closure is available.
Closure is indeed available. It is available as well at West-
minster and available in most other parliaments. But it does
not in these places stand alone. It does not stand alone because its very clumsiness, its time-consuming procedures, demand that it be used only infrequently.
House of Commons, 24 July 1969

In the present dialogue with youth, we must not reply to criticism with reaction but rather with the understanding that
there exists now a need as never before for strong and effective government; government able to respond to the dangers
of the present ideological struggle, to the competition within
our pluralistic societies, to the economic disparities of an un-
balanced world community. We must respond not only with
efficiency and effectiveness and honesty, but with imagination
and sensitivity. To do so requires a combination of listening
and learning, of leading and managing, of governing and
doing.

We must demonstrate that we are capable of devising institutional means which can realize goals of maximum human
dignity, maximum human welfare, maximum environmental
quality, and minimum violence in human relationships. In
short, we must be relevant. Our efforts must be directed not to
the tasks for which government was thought to be designed at
the beginning of the century, but to the tasks for which it must
be designed at the conclusion of the century.

These challenges in the modern world we welcome and accept. A challenge that is more troublesome comes from
within. It is a compound of the heightened expectations of our
citizens, of the despair of young people at the inability of government to meet these expectations, and of the desire of so
many to participate meaningfully in the democratic process.
The challenge is the disenchantment felt by many persons to-

wards government and governmental institutions.

The disenchantment is not ours alone. It is as prevalent in the socialist as in the democratic states; it troubles the leaders of the newly independent countries as much as the leaders of the older nations. This disenchantment with government is not only widespread; it is new. During the first six decades of this century, no problem appeared too complex for government, no instrument was thought better designed to organize and direct for the common good the energies of society than was government. Yet in the past ten years there has arisen doubt and mistrust, and in some instances rebellion, against the concept that government is superbly suited to resolve conflict, to reach decisions and to accomplish good. Gone is the old idea that government could eliminate the evil represented by so-called 'vested interests'; youth all too often now regard government as the biggest of the vested interests, as the symbol of the modern establishment.

As turnabout as this attitude may seem, there is nonetheless something essentially consistent about it. The romantic belief of young people in the 1930s that strong government would eliminate the inequalities brought about by selfish capitalist forces lead for a brief period to a shocking acceptance of the totalitarian forces then emerging in some countries. This theoretic motivation proved to be a romantic escape from the realities of politics and from responsibility. Forty years later the young are against government rather than for it; they are hardened veterans of *realpolitik*, not students of textbook fantasies; yet many of them are equally as irresponsible in a political sense as were their forebears of the thirties. Some of today's youth advocate dropping out. Infatuated with Marcuse, inspired by McLuhan, they are resentful of the record of government.

There is no doubt, however, which of the two generations is more perceptive in its attitude. In the forty-year interval from 1930 to 1970, governments have proved to be all too fallible. All too often governments have tended to over-react and to under-achieve. The young people, who unlike their elders, are not influenced by a long-lasting love affair with government, now often view it as a monstrous, ineffective, costly, disorganized and impotent force.

This is not to say that youth do not believe in the need for government. Far from it. In my experience, youth are articulate in their criticism, but are at the same time almost passionate in their desire to learn and to serve. They view engagement as not only necessary but as the source of adventure as well. Though disenchanted with government performance, they are committed to matters of social concern. Though critical of government policies, they are stout defenders of individual liberty and are tolerant of dissent. As leaders of government we should be grateful for their qualities. We must accept and employ their energy.

Parliamentary Lunch, Canberra, Australia, 19 May 1970

The goals of this Liberal Government have been stated many times, and are best described in terms of an ongoing process:
to preserve our sovereignty and independence;
to work for peace and security;
to promote social justice;
to enrich the quality of life;
to maintain a harmonious natural environment; and
to encourage a prosperous economy.
The pursuit of these goals is not an end in itself; it develops and strengthens the fibre of the Canadian fabric; it contributes to national unity; it makes Canada a better place in which to live.

Liberal Policy Conference, 20 November 1970

Following the pattern of all extremist groups, governments are described as non-representative by persons who claim through some undisclosed authorization to be themselves truly representative of all the members of their generation, or their linguistic group, or their sex. There is nothing new in this respect, it appears, I was amused to learn that in 1912 Sir Rodmond Roblin (then Premier of Manitoba) complained that he was 'opposed by all the short-haired women and the long-haired men in the province'.

Toronto & District Liberal Association, 3 March 1971

The purpose of the federal government is not the accumulation of money or other assets. The federal government does not exist as an entity apart from Canadians. The money it spends in Nova Scotia benefits Nova Scotians – as in the naval dockyards and the Canadian Armed Forces bases, in the modern international airport, in the Halifax harbour facilities, and in dozens of other instances. The role of the federal government then is to lend unity to Canada, to act as supplier of national services, to offer economic stability to those regions which are less wealthy – as the Maritime provinces still are. The federal government is not in competition with provincial governments. Where conflicts occur, they should be resolved not in favour of one level of government or the other but in favour of Canada and Canadians. A stronger Nova Scotia means a stronger Canada.

Nova Scotia Liberal Association, Halifax, 29 October 1971

I just can't understand those who say that the executive of the country is too strong. We haven't destroyed any of the counterweights; we've given more instruments to the opposition to combat us if they want; we've given privileges to the opposition; we've given them research groups; we've given them assistance in all kinds of ways; we have, as you say, provided days where they would be able to move non-confidence motions at regular intervals.

We've tried to provide the counterweights, but I have never said that I want to have a weak government. If this is what you want, I can have six people in my office – I won't be able to follow any of the complex subjects which are being discussed in this government or in this country, and you will have a lousy, weak-kneed government. And if that's the kind of a thing that you want, you had better elect somebody else. I just don't understand this, this absurd criticism of the executive being too strong. I just don't understand it. I have tried in every way to strengthen the Parliament, by setting up committee systems, so the parliamentarians could specialize in certain areas, so that they could divide their time between subjects, so that they could travel around the country, so that they could hear witnesses and receive briefs. I've tried to strengthen Parliament, but I have not tried to weaken the executive and I don't apologize for that.

Interview for CTV with Tom Gould and Bruce Phillips, Ottawa, 28 December 1971

If law is to retain its legitimacy as an important social institution, it must reflect changing values ... A constraint in this respect that has faced all governments in all times, I am sure, is the gap between generations and the difficulty which this gap introduces into any search for a national consensus. That generation gap is still with us but it is reflected now in terms of ideas more than age, and they are turning over at a bewildering pace. No longer can we measure generations in segments of twenty or thirty years; the life-span of an idea or attitude, and often even of some values, is now in many instances not more than five years. Yet our normal legislative cycle for the processing of law from proposal to statute often approaches that same length of time. Just as the pace of technology may make a new machine obsolete almost before it is manufactured, so the speed of new ideas may make some of our laws irrelevant even before they are proclaimed. Laws or institutions regarded as just today will undoubtedly be criticized for their shortcomings next year or the year after. Yet legislatures often approach their task as if their laws would last forever, and as if the legislative process could proceed dreamily at a pace that was sufficient at the turn of the century. Aware of the danger that the public would come to scorn a body incapable of dealing with the needs of the country adequately and in time, the government streamlined some of the procedures of Parliament two years ago. We recognize, however, that much remains to be done.

National Conference on the Law, Ottawa, 1 February 1972

The role of law

Perhaps a good place to begin is to ask what role we think the law should play in Canada? Is it to be, as it so often now *seems* to be, little more than a set of rules which regulate our activities; a body of statutes and judicial decisions which act as precedents for our conduct? Do we give the impression of persons constantly looking backward over our shoulders, attempting to see what was done in the past? The law by this definition is static; rather than *serving* us, we find that it *controls* us. It is a rigid framework within which we must remain, an inflexible harness which binds us to the *status quo* and intimidates our attempts at change. Surely this is not the proper role of the law.

Properly employed, law is the instrument which will permit the preservation of our traditions and the pursuit of the ideals which our society cherishes.

These ideals, or values, are many, but the most basic of them, I suggest, are the freedom and the dignity of the individual. If we, as individuals, do not have the opportunity to stand erect, to retain our self-respect, to move freely throughout our country unhindered by any artificial impediment, then we have not created in this land the political climate that we are capable of creating. We will not have made use of the law as we should.

Constitutional Conference, Ottawa, 5–7 February 1968

On Parliament Hill, 1969

Justice is something we should not feel, justice is something that should exist without us knowing about it. When we talk about justice, it is because there is not enough of it. Justice is something that should go around in disguise, meddling, mixing in the crowd. Justice is something that should be there, and this is the kind of society we want.

Applewood Shopping Plaza, Toronto, 14 June 1968

I repeat, Mr Speaker, these innovations and reforms in the area of criminal law are in some cases overdue. Many of them are in response to demands which have been voiced in an inarticulate but nevertheless sincere fashion by Canadians, young and old, in all walks of life. All of them reflect governmental sensitivity to, and an attempt to understand and rectify, the underlying social causes of crime and disorder. Not surprisingly, their very novelty makes them offensive to some. But their existence on the statute books of Canada is proof that this country is responsive to the needs for social change and is committed to an atmosphere of freedom.

It is important that this be understood by everyone in Canada, Mr Speaker.

Canadians should know that this government will control and restrict within its competence any state activity which interferes unduly with individual liberty. We continue to believe that a constitutionally entrenched charter of human rights of the sort proposed last year will serve as a solid base of human values. In these areas of civil liberties, no government in the world is more sympathetic or more active.

I say this, Mr Speaker, to emphasize that there is no need anywhere in Canada for misguided, or misinformed, zealots to resort to acts of violence in the belief that only in this fashion can they accomplish change. There may be some places in the world where the law is so inflexible and so insensitive as to prompt such beliefs. But Canada is not the place. Those who would defy the law and ignore the opportunities available to them to right their wrongs and satisfy their complaints will receive no hearing from this government. I say to them that the law enforcement agencies in this country are instruments of government. They are responsible to government and answerable for their activities. This being so I emphasize that unlawful acts of violence perpetrated for any reason will be regarded by this government as without excuse and not to be condoned.

My government has no intention of bending before any real or pretended back-lash to so-called 'soft' criminal laws. We are not prepared to back into an authoritarian era because of the activities of a small number of criminally inclined persons. But under no circumstances are we going to permit these same persons to assume that this society will tolerate their criminal activities.

We intend to ensure that the laws Parliament passes are worthy of respect.

And we intend to use our powers to ensure that those laws are respected.

Lest these self-styled Robin Hoods and revolutionaries and romantics have any doubts about the result of their activities, let them be told that anarchy is a two-way street; that in a jungle community there is no dispensation for the property or the lives of hoodlums and thugs, or of so-called activists parading in the guise of taxi drivers or students; none either for their loved ones, or for any other member of the community. In the absence of respect for the law we all stand naked and vulnerable ...

Those who disrespect legal processes expose themselves to still another danger: the danger that law-abiding elements in society will, out of anger for those incidents and out of fear for their own safety, harden their attitudes and refuse to accommodate any changes, or remedy any shortcomings.
House of Commons, 24 October 1969

Q   Did it ever occur to you, as it clearly occurred to this critic, that [criminal sexual] reform would have the overall effect of undermining the general morality of the society and in particular of undermining the family structure, which I think is something which worries people in New Zealand when these sorts of reforms are suggested?
A   Well, I can't say I didn't consider it. I know that it is impossible to draw an absolute impermeable line between your private life and your public conduct, and if people are degenerates in their private life they may be poorer citizens for that.

But what I was essentially saying is that one is not a degenerate just because somebody else says so. There are standards of conduct obviously in societies, for instance in the area of homosexuality, which are not an invention of the twentieth century and which have been existing for a long time, and I don't think that you can legislate them out of existence. You can legislate public effects of certain conduct and prohibit doing things in public, for instance, which are shocking and repulsive to the people of the society in which you live. But what happens in private, once again, is a matter of your relations with your own God and your own internal values. And I think that it is more destructive of a society to force people to live as hypocrites and to respect a morality in which they don't believe for metaphysical or ethical reasons and to have a certain outward conduct because the majority of the people say this is right and this is wrong in moral terms. I think a society can be just as badly maimed by hypocrisy as by these private codes of conduct which don't overflow.

Interview, TV program 'Gallery', New Zealand Broadcasting Commission, Wellington, NZ, 14 May 1970

The liberal philosophy sets the highest value on the freedom of the individual, by which we mean the total individual, the individual as a member of a society to which he is inextricably bound by his way of life, and by community of interest and culture. For a liberal, the individual represents an absolute personal value; the human person has a transcending social significance. Concern for the human person is thus at its most intense within the liberal mind. The tolerance of a liberal man is exemplary. It forbids him any action, or attitude, or omission, that might tend to jeopardize the rights of other individuals.

It is here that the liberal confronts his primordial responsibility: individual freedom. The first visible effect of freedom is change. A free man exercises his freedom by altering himself and – inevitably – his surroundings. It follows that no liberal can be other than receptive to change and highly positive and active in his response to it, for change is the very expression of freedom.

Clearly, though, a liberal can neither encourage nor accept indiscriminate change by indiscriminate means.

The liberal man marks a juncture in human evolution; a point at which social change through violence has become morally unacceptable to many, many people. Violence is the negation of individual rights, and respect for those rights is compatible only with gradual social change through selective and deliberate evolution. No other form of change is worthy of men who have evolved, through liberal thought, to that level at which a growing proportion of mankind claims to function.

That, then, is the liberal responsibility. We are responsible for ensuring the opportunity to evolve in freedom. We are the instigators and the guardians of social evolution. We cannot rest content in benevolent contemplation of change. A passive liberal reclining on the cushions of the liberal tradition is as worthless and ineffective as any spiritless conservative.

The liberal responsiblity must be a warm living thing within us. Life is confrontation, and vigilance, and a fierce struggle against any threat of intrusion or death. We are unworthy of our ideal if we are not ready to defend, as we would life itself, the only roads to change that respect the human person. We are equally unworthy if we are not able to harden ourselves temporarily, but for as long as may be necessary – however repugnant it may be to do so – in order to safeguard and strengthen the contemporary pinnacle of human evolution.

This conception of our responsibility to the individual and to society is in keeping with the vision of the state and its role held by Emmanuel Mounier, a thinker who has had a profound influence on so many men of my generation. 'The role of the state', he said, 'is limited to guaranteeing the fundamental rights of the individual, and placing no obstacle in the path of free competition between schools of thought. The state is nonetheless obligated to guarantee these fundamental rights of the perso. . The performance of this service justifies compulsion in specific circumstances.' According to Mounier, an invariable characteristic of such circumstances is the existence of a threat to personal rights. Any such threat can only be the result of regression.

However great has been human progress in some areas,

mankind is not yet sufficiently homogeneous to be entirely immune to regression. Our own country even now is grappling
with a savage attempt at regression. The violence done to us is
not new; it has overshadowed men from the earliest glimmer
of prehistory; like magic and superstition, it is of the most
primitive stuff of mankind.

The terrorists cannot accept human dignity, nor can they
adapt to the patient workings of the democratic process that
translate our respect for that dignity; they are throwbacks, obsolete dark vestiges of prehistoric animals who bear the traces
of a world predating love and charity.

These tailings of history now know that we shall not permit
the destruction of a country that stands as an example and an
inspiration to our times, a country that is for Canadians a
great and strong abode of freedom and hope.
Liberal Policy Conference, 20 November 1970

My whole position on morality versus criminality is that the
criminal law should not be used to express the morality of any
one group, religious or pressure groups, or others. The criminal law is not made to punish sin, it is meant to prevent or deter anti-social conduct. And this is a question not of religion;
it is a question of public morality.
Mount Royal Liberal Association, Montreal, 25 November 1971

The constitution

I have been asked what need there is in Canada for a bill of
rights. My answer is that our need may not be so great as is
that of persons in some other countries. But my answer as well
is that we should not over-emphasize our righteousness. We
are not in this country innocent of book-burning or -banning
legislation, of deprivations by law of previously guaranteed
minority language rights, of legal expropriation which at times
appears to be more akin to confiscation, of persons arrested in
the night and held incommunicado for days. We have no reason to be complacent. How many Canadians know that Canadian law permits evidence to be introduced by the police into
criminal trials no matter how illegally that evidence may have
been obtained? Apart from confessions, for which there are
elaborate rules to ensure that they are voluntary, incriminating
evidence is admissible in our courts no matter how obtained.
It may have been gained by fraud, the law enforcement agencies may have stolen it; they may have obtained it without a
search warrant, or by means of breaking and entering private
premises. To the great credit of the police forces of this country, these tactics are seldom employed. But do we wish to live
in a country where they may be employed? And where on occasion they are employed? Where one standard of conduct is
expected of citizens and another permitted of government agencies?

I do not, and it is my guess that the great number of Canadians do not.

I ask you as well to consider that this is a Canadian Charter [of Human Rights] for Canadian circumstances. I am aware of the criticism from some quarters in the United States of some of the results of American civil rights legislation, and I am aware that some of the initial opposition in this country to a Bill of Rights was based upon the evidence of American experience. It would be unfortunate if our criticism of some aspects of American society caused us to forget that there has been created in the United States one of the great legal systems of the world. In our natural desire to borrow some of what is good from that system, we should not be inhibited by those who warn us of what is bad. We are aware of some of its shortcomings; I simply say that the American precedent with respect to those shortcomings is not valid in Canada.

Canadians are not prone to acts of violence. Our police enjoy on the whole the respect of the people. We find abhorrent the 'shoot-to-kill' legislation which permits some policemen elsewhere to attack lethally criminal suspects who are running away. Our courts function differently from those in many other countries. Canadian lawyers owe a duty not only to their client and to society but to the courts as well for they are 'officers of the court', and subject to the court's contempt sanctions. They are also subject to the vigorous discipline of their own professional societies. Criminal prosecutions are not generally in Canada a game between an elected prosecutor and a flamboyant defence counsel, as can happen elsewhere. The rules of procedure in Canadian courts differ from those, for example, in other countries, and the exclusion of evidence by an appellate court will not necessarily result in a quashed conviction and a repetition of the entire trial procedure.

In short, we should not underestimate the strengths of our society and assume that the public interest will automatically suffer if the interest of the individual is further protected.

I wish to make it clear that in proposing [the Canadian Charter of Human Rights] there is no suggestion that the federal government is seeking any power at the expense of the provinces. We are stating that we are willing to *surrender* some of our power to the people of Canada, and we are suggesting that the provincial governments surrender some of *their* power to the people in the respective provinces. It is because we are a federal state, with competence to legislate divided between provincial governments and the federal government, that we must *all* act in order effectively to protect *all* of the rights of *all* of the people.

Admittedly, some aspects of these rights fall within the exclusive legislative competence of Parliament, some aspects fall within the exclusive competence of the provinces, and some are subject to shared competence. There is no intention that the federal government use its criminal law powers as a means of invading provincial jurisdiction. Indeed quite the contrary. An examination of the categories of all fundamental rights, however described, for which we propose protection, reveals that the bulk of them fall now under federal jurisdiction. This means that in this process of surrender of power that we are proposing, Parliament will be giving up far more than will the provinces. There is no transfer, no delegation, no encroachment from one level of government to another. The items in the Charter which are properly within provincial jurisdiction remain there and remain subject to *provincial* and not federal sanctions. Some items, particularly those involving linguistic rights, will require co-operation. It *is* evidence that a single, constitutional Canadian Charter of Human Rights is required in order to deal adequately in this federal state, Canada, with the protection of human rights.

How best do we form a constitution which will contain the framework necessary to support a federal structure and which, at the same time, will be sensitive to the need for change, and responsive to it?

Do we first argue about the rights of governments and carefully compartmentalize Canada into parts, building tough exteriors about the governments to ensure that each is guarded effectively from outside interference? Would this achieve our purpose? Would the people of Canada accept the proposition that omnipotent governments are best for them?

Or do we attempt to construct a Canada in which the prime strength is not in the governments, but in the people; a country which is knit together from coast to coast by persons confident of their individual rights wherever they may live; a

At a sugaring-off party, St Joseph-du-Lac, March 1971

Canada with which the people may identify, and in which they will then be given a voice to decide the competence which their governments should possess?

The first technique has been tried again and again for decades by those who argue that stronger federal, or stronger provincial, governments will guarantee utopia. How often have we witnessed governments arguing about distribution of power? And yet we sit here today cognizant of discontent in Canada. I ask you to consider a new approach. An approach which deals first and foremost with the *people* of Canada.

If we look to nature, we may find examples of the two forms of structure. Those creatures which are of the crustacean species have armoured themselves against the outside; all sensitivity and life is confined to the interior of the shell where it is free from harm and immune from most danger. The opposite structure is found in vertebrates where a strong skeletal framework is inside, not outside. In this species the flesh is constantly exposed to danger – but it is at the same time not immune from its environment. It is capable of adaptation, of change, of more advanced forms of life.

I suggest that the vertebrate provides us with a better example. That we here today have the opportunity of starting to build a new constitutional structure for Canada; one which is strong because its backbone is composed of human beings secure in their individual liberty and confident of the protection of their fundamental values.

Knowing, whether they be Manitobans, Quebeckers, or Prince Edward Islanders, that they have common values, that they are united in these respects as *Canadians* – not divided provincially by differences – this is the strength of Canada. And if this structure exposes our cultures to some danger, should we not accept the challenge? Great cultures have always flourished when they have been forced to, but many have suffocated when over-protected.

Constitutional Conference, Ottawa, 5–7 February 1968

In February of 1968 there was unanimity in recognizing the perils that were besetting Confederation, and in the importance of identifying and offsetting those perils by constitutional means. I have no hesitation in saying, Mr Speaker, that the importance of this task of constitutional review has not lessened in the past twelve months. Nor do I hesitate to say that in my belief the task is even more urgent now than it was when we began a year ago. It would be folly of the most dangerous sort for us in 1969 to persuade ourselves that the discontent in French Canada which we all recognized in 1968 – and the causes of which the first session of the conference dedicated itself to removing – has in any appreciable measure disappeared. It would be hypocritical of us as legislators if we assumed, in the face of the steadily mounting evidence to the contrary in our society, that the individual human being needs no protection of his basic rights against the inroads of governments and the bureaucratic institutions and agencies which governments spawn. It would be an act of irresponsibility if we accepted the simplistic argument that there is nothing wrong with Canada that a revision of revenue-sharing would not correct.

Prime Minister Pearson stated last February that at stake in this sweeping process of constitutional review and reform was nothing less than Canada's survival. I would not be candid if I did not say that today, one year later, the stake has not in my opinion changed. Canada's survival remains in issue.

If we are not able to take whatever steps are necessary to provide in this country equality of opportunity to all Canadians – equality which reveals no exceptions based on use of either of the official languages, or on regional economic disparities, or on basic individual freedoms – then we shall have failed. We shall have disappointed the expectations of the Fathers of Confederation. And we shall have disappointed as well the expectations of persons in many other countries who regard Canada as an example of a workable federal system in a co-operating bilingual community.

I believe that we shall not fail. I believe that we are capable of meeting successfully the challenge that faces us, which is no less than a systematic and comprehensive review of the structural framework of our Canadian society.

House of Commons, 6 February 1969

Q How long will the monarchy last for Canadians?
A Well, you're asking me how long this government will last.

The monarchy will last as long as this government lasts. Now what happens if somebody else is elected, I just can't predict. But I have stated quite clearly that this government had no mandate to abolish the monarchy and didn't intend doing so. But if somebody else is elected on a platform of abolishing the monarchy, then it will be abolished.

Q   As the expert on French Canada, sir ...

A   Thank you very much.

Q   ... can you tell me if the monarchy is a sore, part of the separatism problem in French Canada? Is it part of the problem? Would it help if the monarchy were to go quietly away ...

A   I don't think so.

Q   ... for national unity?

A   I don't think so. I have no hesitation in saying that the separatists themselves do make this an issue and say: we need a republic and not a monarch, not a Queen. But the separatists are out to destroy the country by definition; therefore I discount their opinion as regards the future of the country. So long as the rest of the French Canadians are concerned, I don't think that they are loyal to the monarchy in the same sense that the English Canadians are, I should say some or many English Canadians. They are, shall we say, more passive towards the institution. I think that they respect the symbol but they don't have a particularly warm feeling towards the individual of the Queen.

Q   You, yourself, are a confirmed monarchist, is that right? Do I gather correctly?

A   I, myself, believe that the simplest and best solution now for Canada is to preserve the monarchy, for a very simple process: that if we were, for the sake of argument, to want to eliminate the monarchy we would be replacing it by what? By an elected president, I suppose.

Q   One of the things I would like to pick up on is the fact that the parliamentary committee on the Constitution has been discussing the possibility of abolition of the monarchy and turning into a republic. Would I be safe to say then that if this Committee did report in that way that you would not accept that as a mandate or a guide to the government for behaviour?

A   Yes, it would be fair to say that. The government's position was made quite clear in a white paper which we submitted to the Constitutional Conference in 1968 and again in 1969, 'The Constitution and the People of Canada'. We declared quite clearly that the new constitution of Canada, if we were to have our way, would be a monarchy and the head of state would be the Queen or the King. So the government is on record for more than two years as that being its position. Now, if Parliament, hypothetically, if the committee of Parliament comes up with that report, it will be up to Parliament to confirm or deny the recommendations of that report and your guess is as good as mine as to what they would do ... So I can only give you the government's position. I can't predict what would happen either in a vote in the House which went against the government or, as Mr Webster was putting it, if there were a general election and a party were elected on the platform of abolishing the monarchy.

Interview on 'Weekend', CBC-TV, *16 May 1971*

One part of our task today is with us because Canada blazed a trail that many former colonies, now independent countries, have since followed. Canada was the first part of the then British Empire that achieved the status that grew into the complete independence of today. The other British colonies that much later achieved independence profited by our experience. They were set up in the world complete – able to manage and to amend their own constitutions. The Fathers of Confederation at Charlottetown and at Quebec, were men of courage, imagination and resource. But neither they nor the British legislators of that day could be expected to have foreseen the way in which complete independence would come to Canada more than half a century later. Because of that they did not include in our constitution a way to amend it in Canada. And so today, a century later, we still cannot change in Canada the fundamental aspects of our constitution. Australia can. New Zealand can. India, Nigeria, Jamaica – all these former British colonies, now independent, can amend their own constitutions in entirety, but we cannot. We Canadians, who led the way, must go to the British Parliament to implement our decision.

Constitutional Conference, Victoria, BC, *14 June 1971*

For Human
Benefit

The economy

Q Mr Prime Minister, what is the Canadian government's
policy with regard to foreign investment in Canada? Do you
foresee controls or limitations on future capital imports?
A No, I do not. The Canadian government's policy on foreign economic investment is that Canada needs foreign investment in order to develop. The point is that this foreign investment should be directed by Canadian governments, not controlled; but it should be encouraged in areas which are conducive to the political and social goals of all of Canada.

We have in this country a limited amount of savings; therefore we have limited investment possibilities of our own. The
important thing is not to frighten away foreign capital investment. This is very easy to do. As I said before, Cuba could do
it in three weeks; we could do it even more quickly, if we
wanted. You can get rid of foreign capital much too easily for
it to be safe. What is important is not to get rid of foreign capital, it is perhaps to diversify it more; and we are doing this
now by borrowing not only in the United States market, but
presently in the German market; and within a month or two
you will see other Canadian borrowings in other European
markets. Therefore, we must diversify foreign investment in
Canada, and we must especially use our own savings, our own
investments, and channel them, as I said tonight, into these
areas which are crucial to the future economic growth of this

Drum-dancing at Baker Lake, NWT, March 1970

country. We should not attempt so much to get rid of foreign
capital by buying back our industries as to make sure that
what money, what savings, what investment possibilities we
have are directed not, once again, towards buying back the
past, but towards buying up the future. We should as Canadians concentrate on this rather than worrying about our prosperity.

Kitchener Chamber of Commerce, Kitchener, Ont., 21 May 1968

Q   Mr Prime Minister, I would like to know how and when
you are going to sell the Western Canadian farmers' wheat?
A   Well, why should I sell the Canadian farmers' wheat? You
know, the way I understand the system, the Canadian farmer
has been very productive, very progressive, and very aggres-
sive. He has increased his productivity enormously. He has
founded co-operatives, he has organized the Wheat Board –
which is not a political instrument once again, it is something
which I think belongs as much to the farmers as to the Canadian government – and he has chosen to operate in a free market economy. He is entitled, I think, the wheat farmer, to as
much protection from the Canadian government as other pro-
ducers get in other countries with whom he has to be in competition. And there are various forms of assistance. I shouldn't
be telling this out in the West – I am only beginning to learn
these things. But there are crop insurances, and there are advance payments and there is PFRA to help land assembly and
irrigation and so on. There are various ways in which the state
does intervene to help the farmer in distress. But every time
there is a drought in another country and we sell more, or
every time the other countries produce more and they don't
have to buy as much from Canada, or every time that our produce is not competitive with produce of other countries, which
perhaps sell different kinds of wheat which are cheaper and of
which you can produce more per acre, it's all of Canada's
problem because the wheat is so important to the Canadian
economy. But it is first and foremost the farmer's problem. He
makes his representations known, believe me, through his
members of Parliament. We hear them every day and that is
right. But I think that we all realize that, as in the case of

other sectors of the economy, the alternative is for the state to
be the producer, to own the land, to own the wheat, to hire
the farmers and to pay them a wage, and then it will be our
problem to sell it and market it. But if we want to have something of a free economy, we can assist – as we do politically –
the farmer in various ways; we can also perhaps encourage or
hopefully prod sometimes the Wheat Board. But the Wheat
Board, I think on balance – and you would say this perhaps
more than I – has done a very good job of selling our wheat.
In cases where we cannot sell it, we make it part of our external aid program. I believe the Minister of External Affairs will
announce next week, if I am allowed to scoop him, that there
will be 15 million bushels of wheat offered to India under our
external aid program. I know that there was some wheat given
to the Niger and to the Ivory Coast, though there is some
question whether the Ivory Coast really wants it or not. You
know these are forms – ways – in which the Canadian government can help the problem when there is a great problem. But
basically unless you take the view that the government should
step in and own the farms and hire the farmers, I think we all
share the responsibility and we will all have to do the best we
can all together.

Liberal Party In Manitoba, Winnipeg, 13 December 1968

Q   Your battle against inflation: who is that battle to benefit,
the sort of comfortable middle class of the country or is it to
benefit the poor of the country?
A   If you want to know the answer, ask yourself whom
inflation hurts most. Inflation hurts most those people who are
less able to defend themselves against the consequences of
inflation; those people who are on fixed incomes, that is the
pensioners, the retired, the aged people or those who are
infirm in one way or another, those who are not members of a
strong economic group; companies or owners ... can always
get around inflation by increasing their rents or their professional fees or the price of their products. Even the workers in
strong trade unions can protect themselves quite easily against
inflation by banding together as they do and bargaining very
toughly with the big companies and making sure they are as

far ahead of the game as they can be. So whom does inflation hurt most? It hurts the little people, the people who don't belong to big unions, who don't belong to big corporations, who are on fixed incomes, or who are workers in either weak unions or ununionized sections of the society. These are the people who are hurt by inflation and these are the people also who will be hit hardest by unemployment if as a result of inflation the Canadian economy loses its grip on some of its foreign market.

Q Sir, at the same time you stated that you are willing to accept 6 per cent unemployment and that's falling right into all these terrible conditions which you have just elucidated on.

A But you see the choice isn't between inflation or unemployment. The choice is that if you have inflation you have, as I said, increasing unemployment and you have the weakening of the whole society, of the whole value of your dollar. Therefore, the choice is between: fighting inflation and eventually strengthening, not only the little man, the unprotected, but the economy to boot; or not fighting inflation and then let everyone who can run faster than inflation, those who are strong and able and who can defend themselves, keep ahead of the game, to the eventual result that the little poor people will be left further and further behind. That is the choice.

CBC - TV *'Under Attack', Carleton University, 24 February 1970*

Environmental consequences, once almost totally overlooked, are becoming more widely understood and in the result compensated or corrected. Less understood, perhaps, is the long-range damage not to the environment, but to the economy, through the tolerance and even the encouragement of another type of industry – the old-fashioned, often inefficient, but usually labour-intensive industry. In order to compete even in domestic markets these industries, often producing relatively unsophisticated products, require tariff protection and artificial help. What begins as an apparently reasonable step – the protection of jobs in a given industry – has far-reaching effects, often bad. Other countries are then more inclined to erect tariff barriers to protect their inefficient industries, and by so doing close their markets to competition from Canadian products. The countries which suffer most from the exclusion of products are often the very countries which Canada is trying to help through our economic assistance programs; countries such as Singapore or Jamaica which have not yet developed a sophisticated technology and so are forced to depend upon the less complicated manufacturing processes as the first step in their climb towards economic self-sufficiency.

Too little heed has been paid in the past to such considerations as these in governmental attempts to attract or develop industry. I am hopeful that more will be paid in the future; that efforts to broaden the economic base of the Maritime provinces, for example, will be selective and forward-looking. Our goal should be factories prepared to manufacture goods of the future, in ways that protect the environment for the future. We must emphasize productivity and efficiency, not tariffs and protection. We must not neglect either cost effectiveness of the activity, or the potential burden upon society of the product.

There should be little doubt that we are capable of meeting (market) challenges. Our own manufacturing potential has recently proved that, under favourable circumstances, it can compete with the world. We need only look back a few years at our merchandise trade account for proof. In the period 1953-58 the goods *deficit* averaged $300 million annually; in the period 1961-70 this became an average *surplus* in the neighbourhood of $700 million. This was an almost incredible turnaround of some billion dollars annually. This record was possible largely because of the widening supply capability of Canadian industry and the growing confidence on the part of Canadian businessmen in their ability to compete internationally. It is proof of the aggressiveness and competence of Canadian entrepreneurs and of the skills and productivity of the Canadian work force.

I sense here tonight a similar confidence. We have shown to the world our ability to compete in manufactured goods; we have proven to ourselves and to the world our ability to achieve price stability. Of all industrialized nations of the western world, Canada's record in battling inflation is unsurpassed, according to figures collected by OECD. We must now seize the opportunity which these advantages confer upon us and move towards the goal of an economy which offers full employment and which will eliminate the vicious and un-wholesome regional disparities now with us.

These things we can do. Discipline is required, and perse-verence: traits which Canadians surely have in abundance. And imagination.

Service Club Council of Saint John, N B, *8 December 1970*

The issues underlying the present state of the Canadian econ-omy are not ones of compassion; surely it would be hard to find anywhere in Canada a person not moved by the plight of those unable to find work. The issue is one of jobs, and of the freedom which any Canadian government is able to exercise in its attempts to encourage a healthy economy and a high rate of employment.

The challenge is to remedy the wrongs and to assist the in-jured. Neither the unemployment situation nor the economic problems which Canada faces will be solved without an honest appreciation of circumstances, however.

In Canada, we are confronted by a number of continuing facts of life which contribute to winter unemployment, to the costs of production and to the costs of government. We should face them squarely.

Firstly, we are visited annually by one of the most severe winters found anywhere in the world. Our climate imposes seasonal limitations on outdoor activity and, in the result, on the number of jobs which can be performed during winter months. For this reason, our winter unemployment figures will always run at a higher rate than those, for example, in the United States where winters are less severe. Though there are some steps which can be taken, and are being taken to offset these effects, we shall always have with us in Canada a num-ber of persons in certain categories who are unable to pursue their livelihood in the winter and who become unemployed automatically. Fishermen and some construction workers are good examples.

Secondly, we are a small population spread across an im-mense land mass with all of the marketing, transportation and communications problems which flow from that fact. We are, for example, the only industrialized country in the world which does not have favoured or immediate access to markets of 100 or more million people. In the result, unit costs of production are high.

Thirdly, partly because of our frontier spirit and partly because of a highly developed sense of social justice shared by most Canadians – both long evident in this province – we find in Canada a broad, advanced and expensive social security system which requires constant attention and servicing. Our new unemployment insurance plan is more liberal than any similar plan on this continent. The result? Governments require a good deal of tax revenue.

Fourthly, we are geographically adjacent to the world's most powerful economic giant, with all of the resulting advantages and disadvantages. Any disturbance in the American economy is soon felt on this side of the border, be it in the form of recession, unemployment, balance of payments problems, inflation, or otherwise. Over the years, American and Canadian business cycles have closely paralleled one another. We cannot always in Canada pick and choose among the effects of the United States economy. It is false, for example, to think that we can permit without resistance the effects of American inflation and yet somehow or other, at the same time, prevent the spread into Canada of American unemployment pressures.

There is a fifth factor, of more recent origin. The number of persons entering the Canadian work force for the first time each year is substantially higher than in most other western countries. For example, employment – not unemployment, but employment, the number of persons working – rose considerably faster in Canada in 1970 than it did in any of the other industrialized countries, including the United States. Our labour force is growing at an extremely rapid rate – about 3 per cent annually in the past three years, and requires the creation in Canada of an immense number of new jobs each year just to keep unemployment figures static. That number is in excess of 200,000.

None of these factors, nor others that I could list, came upon us without warning in the past year. None of them eases

At a Liberal dinner, Quebec City, November 1971

the pain felt by any one unemployed person. None of them can or will be used by the federal government as an argument with which to excuse the very disturbing unemployment situation now present in Canada. By the same token, however, none of them should be forgotten by those persons who race from coast to coast leaving behind them a trail of inconsistent, unworkable and irresponsible theories as to how they would turn off unemployment for ever and create within Canada a society of low taxes and high welfare, low imports and high exports, low-cost housing and high-price incomes.

At the moment the chief contribution of these persons has been low credibility and high volume.

Inflation of the kind the world is now experiencing has a double kick, and both are aimed at people. The first reduces the buying power of the dollar and makes us all a little bit poorer; the second erodes the vitality of the economy and leads directly to slow-downs and enduring unemployment.

When the government fought inflation, it was fighting the long-term battle against unemployment. Inflation and unemployment are, in the long run, two aspects of the same evil. Had we not taken on that fight, we should have been irresponsible.

Liberal Party of Saskatchewan, Regina, 13 February 1971

Challenge is no stranger to the Canadian entrepreneur. It is challenge that motivates him. His response is innovation. Perhaps nowhere else in the world do instant challenge and sudden opportunity appear so often and so simultaneously as they do in the Canadian market place. On our border is the world's most versatile and capitalized industrial society. The Canadian user and consumer are aware instantly of the accomplishments and the products of American technology and American manufacturers. Canadian demand is encouraged through the same channels employed for the American consumer, and at the same time. The Canadian market expects instantly the same products, with the same performance, the same quality, and the same range of models, colours, accessories and service. Canada is perhaps the only country in the world where manufacturers are unable to plead for time on the grounds of distance from the US, disparity of market circumstances, unlikelihood of product suitability, or need to tool up. If an item appears in an American city, be it a machine tool or a TV dinner, the Canadian consumer expects the same product from his local supplier at the same time.

The history of Canadian manufacturing is the history of industry's response to this kind of sudden demand as much as it is the story of fresh initiatives in a country whose geography, climate and society combine to create peculiar needs for specialized products. It is a tribute to the Canadian businessman that he has acquired a reputation in Canada and throughout the world for design and product quality under these circumstances. The 'Made in Canada' tag is not a symbol of chauvinism, it is a testimonial to reliability and attractiveness.

Canadian Manufacturers' Association, Toronto, 8 June 1971

The economic policies announced last weekend by President Nixon are very complex; their full impact both in the United States and in many other countries will not be known for some time. There is little mystery, however, about the effect on Canada of one of the policies – the 10 per cent import surcharge. If nothing is done to remove or prevent the impact of that surcharge, if it is given full effect, it will cause the loss of many thousands of Canadian jobs.

That is a rough blow to this country. It was to ensure that the United States government was aware of just how rough that Mr Benson and Mr Pepin went to Washington yesterday. They did not go to seek favours, still less to make concessions. They went to make clear to the United States government that there was no justification for what it was doing to Canada. Secretary Connally agreed to give our arguments careful consideration, and we are now awaiting a reply.

Canada, of course, is not the only country that is affected by this particular policy. For that reason we welcome the consultations that will be taking place with other trading nations who share membership with us in the associations which exist for that purpose – the International Monetary Fund, GATT, and the Group of Ten – to see what can be done to achieve the improved international trade and financial arrangements which the US is seeking.

Canada does not take issue with the decision of the United States to grapple with its economic problems. Several of those problems are familiar to us. It is of no less importance to Canada than to the United States that both inflation and unemployment be attacked with vigour. Our message to the United States government is quite simple: we understand your problem, we sympathize wholeheartedly with your goal of a healthy economy, we suggest only that the application of your surcharge to Canadian exports contributes in no way to the attainment of that goal. A weak Canadian economy is no help to the United States. Unemployed Canadians cannot afford to buy US goods. At the present time, as for several years, US exports to Canada are comparable to the combined total of all American sales to Japan, Germany, Britain and France; we buy about one quarter of all US exports. Without our market the US economy would be in much more serious difficulties than it now finds itself.

Canadians enjoy one of the highest standards of living in the world. We do so because of our success as a trading nation. Were we not such strong traders – on a per capita basis, the biggest in the world – our standard of living would be a fraction of what it now is. One quarter of our GNP comes from external trade. We cannot, of course, sit mutely and absorb the impact of this United States surcharge which, if it continues in effect against Canada, will hurt us more than any other country. But neither is it in our interest to retaliate and set in motion the destructive spiral of an international trade war. Everyone would be a loser in those circumstances.

Our policy, then, is to take all steps to dampen elsewhere in the world talk of such a self-defeating practice and to press the United States government to re-examine the surcharge as it applies to us. The United States government has made no complaint to Canada about artificial exchange rates. Nor has it raised with us more than minor matters in respect to Canada's trade practices. There is no justification, therefore, for applying penalties to Canadian trade.

We wish the United States every success in restoring its economy to health. We ask, however, that in meeting unfair

practices on the part of other countries it not itself be unfair. I am confident that President Nixon intended no unfairness and that this problem will be resolved in the spirit of friendship which characterizes all relations between our two countries.
National television broadcast, 20 August 1971

A major factor which must be taken into account in judging the value of the recent discoveries, is the fantastic cost involved in locating, acquiring, and bringing to shore oil found beneath the ocean. In the past ten years the oil industry has spent an estimated $130 million in the search for oil off these shores, and expects to spend a billion more on exploration in the next decade. Exploration at sea is from three to ten times as costly as on shore. Drilling costs show an even greater disparity. In all the world there are only a dozen drilling units capable of operating year round off the Canadian east coast. Three of these are now in use here and another is committed for 1972. To keep one of these rigs in activity requires an expenditure of $30,000 to $40,000 every 24 hours. Much of this money is spent locally, which is of benefit to Nova Scotia, but equally it must be remembered that investment on that scale must be raised before it can be spent.

It has been estimated that the commercial development of an offshore field – when once discovered and explored – will require an investment of between $100 and $250 million to provide the necessary permanent platforms, the production equipment and the gathering system. Transportation of the oil to shore is not included in that figure. A pipeline from Sable Island, for example, might cost as much as $100 million.

How big must an oil-field be before the companies involved will commit themselves to such huge expenditures of funds? The Canadian Petroleum Association estimates that the daily production would have to be in the order of 50,000 to 100,000 barrels of oil in order to justify the investment. Only four oil-fields in Canada at the present time are that big. Canada's largest field is Pembina in Alberta. Notwithstanding the huge size of that field, it would be uneconomic if located offshore because its productive zone is too thin to support the high offshore costs.

I have not recited these figures in order to dampen your enthusiasm as Maritimers. Certainly the oil companies remain enthusiastic, and I find their enthusiasm infectious. If I chose to talk about these facts, to emphasize the nature of this new enterprise in which you are engaged, it's because I want to underline again the importance to Canada in certain industries and regions of foreign capital. Without a continuing positive political climate in Canada, investment of that magnitude would go elsewhere. Canada's east coast shelf is far from being the only attractive offshore site in the eyes of international oil companies. Indeed many other offshore areas are more attractive from the standpoint both of demonstrated reserves and of operating conditions. At the present time there are a number of major areas of activity, including the Gulf of Mexico, the Persian Gulf, the North Sea, and the sea off Indonesia, and there are at least fifty other offshore areas competing for the use of the limited number of drilling units. This is a big business, a global business, one in which both the federal government and the Nova Scotia government have a considerable interest. That interest is complementary and requires the close co-operation of the two governments in order properly to protect and promote the country and the province.

We are very conscious of the need to ensure the maximum possible Canadian content and advantage in all the offshore and onshore activities, both to ensure stable and economic job development in the Maritimes and to protect and preserve the ocean and shore environments. It's not our intention to be so rigid or so demanding as to cause the oil industry to lose interest in this area, but neither are we so unaware of the environmental hazards involved in this kind of activity that we are not firm in our demands for safety and care. The oil industry, I wish to add, is co-operating fully in these respects; it operates in this country under Canadian rules, obeying Canadian tax laws, and susceptible to Canadian sensitivities. It recognizes fully the damage done to it as an industry when error or negligence occurs and injury results as has happened elsewhere. It is the desire of both levels of government, and of industry, to encourage this potential development to become a valuable and responsible reality in order to make available to the markets of Atlantic Canada and Quebec energy from Canadian

sources at a saving in foreign exchange of several hundred millions of dollars per year.
Nova Scotia Liberal Association, Halifax, 29 October 1971

In the very disturbing picture painted by forecasts for the year 2000, agriculture is a crucial factor. By then we must have reached a level of agricultural sufficiency which we can hardly even imagine at present, and agriculture will not be able to meet that challenge if it does not have sufficient human resources and if it does not become economically independent. Like any other industrial sector, it has to operate and will have to operate without subsidies, without outside aid, as a mature organism that has developed to its full potential.

It is less and less acceptable that the consumer should have to bear the cost of deficiencies which the farmer himself suffers, but the consumer must realize how essential is the aid he now gives the farmer through government programs. Subsidies and grants are no longer just stop-gap measures: from now on they will be transitional measures which are part of a long-term rationalization policy.

To gain a sound understanding of our agricultural policy, we must first consider the government's role. This is essentially to provide Canadian agriculture with what it cannot provide for itself, or what a central body can most easily ensure, namely, services and a legal framework conforming to our constitution.

Such a role must be played while actively seeking the overall objective: the establishment of an economic climate favourable to all industrial sectors, one that will enable farmers to reach an average income level comparable to that of other citizens.

In short, what we intend to achieve, here in Quebec as in the rest of Canada, is a viable, profitable, independent and self-sufficient agricultural industry. We believe that this objective corresponds to the desires of all Canadian farmers. We are certain that with a concerted effort by both sides we can make considerable progress in this direction. To reach this objective, changes will no doubt have to be made, since progress and change obviously go hand in hand. Our concern, however, is to ensure that the changes you may desire, as representatives of Canadian agriculture, will be made as efficiently as possible and without unduly upsetting society or the individual.

Since we formed the government, we faced another major problem, that of the transformation of rural society, based in the past on the small farm concept. The fact is that the small farm, even with mechanization, is becoming less and less profitable. Technology and irresistible economic pressures demand land areas much larger than those that supported the old-time farmer. Lacking capital (which he needs more than manpower), the farmer is often unable to adapt to the system; isolated and reduced to poverty, he must, in spite of his deep love for the land, sell it on unfavourable terms and move to an urban environment for which he is unprepared. The rural exodus too often involves farmers who feel a deep sense of tragedy in having to quit their lands. These are unhappy experiences that can be avoided.

The first aim of our Small Farms Development Program announced in December is to give small farmers who want to remain on the farm the means to develop a profitable enterprise. From the outset, it is obvious that our policy greatly favours the family unit, the best way in most cases to operate a farm. Family operation is readily adaptable to farm industrialization; it lends itself well to different forms of co-operation. For example, the co-operative movement possesses an economic efficiency comparable to corporate farming enterprises. It also avoids anonymity, gigantism and the formidable problems of labour common to all large businesses. Even if some concentrations are inevitable in the farm sector, fortunately agriculture is capable of maintaining its innate humanity without sacrificing production. We consider this unique quality of the agricultural community a valuable asset, an important element of social stability and a great cultural advantage.

On the other hand, many farmers want to leave the land, and others, the victims of merciless selection, are forced to leave, however regrettable that may be. It is impossible to stop the rural exodus completely but, in so far as it is inevitable, it can be made more humane: that is a complementary objective of the Small Farms Development Program.

I cannot accept the interpretation of those who persist in seeing this measure as a disguised plan by the government to force small farmers off the land and out of rural areas ... we have no such intention. Though recognizing some instances of hardship we do not desire to make it worse. On the contrary, we are taking steps to alleviate it, to mitigate its effects. Under this program, persons forced to sell will sell to their advantage enabling them to retire with self-respect and, if they so desire, to keep a parcel of land and their home. Is this running people off the land? Others, and they are many, wish to put their talents to good use in activities other than farming and would not be able to do so without the help of the program. Does strengthening the inalienable right of people to change their life style amount to telling them what to do? Furthermore, it will be possible to use the property acquired under the program to set up reserves of desirable farmland which can be used to enlarge small family holdings and establish them on a firmer footing. In this way considerable stretches of land can be returned to their proper use. Can aims such as these be regarded as suspect? One need only look at the facts to realize that this program is a significant step towards furthering social justice.

We must not forget that some of the solutions [to agricultural problems] which are now being applauded result from policies that were, at the outset, unpopular and that we had the courage to enforce. The case of the dairy industry is typical in this respect. As it benefitted from our rationalization policy, we are not hesitating to pursue this policy in other areas. We do not wish to impose rationalization, but rather encourage it by creating conditions conducive to its acceptance. Bill c-176, adopted on December 30, 1971, illustrates this point perfectly: it supplies a rational framework for free initiative. It is not by short term or fleetingly popular measures that we can ensure the progress of the agricultural milieu, but by long-term acts, aimed at the common good: the only acts, in effect, which should win public respect for a government.

The common good requires sustained economic progress accompanied by a gradual sharing of the national wealth. Our entire policy has resulted directly from our conception of the common good, whose underlying principles are growth and redistribution.

The basic indices confirm this growth; the extensive legislation adopted is evidence of redistribution. In our opinion, prosperity and redistribution of goods are based on the same principle of justice. In our political thought, wealth should not be confined, nor should poverty be segregated. Since we seek justice, we want all elements of society to open up to one another.

Coopérative Fédérée de Québec, Montreal, 2 February 1972

At Williams Lake, B C, August 1970

The environment

The modern city can generate feelings of depression and irresponsibility or feelings of well-being and civic pride. It can release the worst in us or it can release the best in us. It can produce, as it has throughout the ages, the most refined civilizations, and it is most of the time in cities that the great inventions and the great discoveries of the mind or of technology have been found. It is through the exchange of men living in cities that the divisions of labour and of trade and of science and the exchange of technologies have permitted mankind to progress, and we must realize that that will be so in the future, but only if we can control our destinies, if we can make sure that we tackle these problems in time. Otherwise we will have to do as some people suggest, just move completely out and start anew in some other place before we can begin again. I hope this will not happen. I hope that for people like yourselves who are struggling with this problem and who are doing so in co-operation with the provincial and the federal levels of government, that we as Canadians can benefit from the experience of others and can apply our own ingenuity to find solutions of our own, and I am confident that we can. In this vast country it is not too late to act. We can still repair some of the shortcomings of the past and we certainly have time to plan for the great urban growth of the future. But the time to act is now.

Canadian Federation of Mayors and Municipalities, Edmonton, 4 June 1968

We know these problems can be solved, but we know that we can only solve them if we act together; and we know, basically, that if we do not manage to re-introduce human values in our cities, if we do not manage to make sure that they grow up on a scale which is conducive to human beings, if we do not make sure that not only we have roofs over our heads, if we do not have park lands in which our children can play, in which the old people can sit in the sun, if we cannot manage to integrate all these areas in the same city in a harmonious way, we know that the values for which we stand will not last.

The cities will preserve democracy or they will not keep democracy and the country will lose it.

City Hall, Toronto, 19 June 1968

The continued growth of our large cities is not a passing phenomenon which will soon disappear, nor is it something about which we should despair. Cities are capable of providing attractive settings in which to work, play and live. There is no reason why any Canadian centre should fall victim to, or remain in the grips of, the paralysis suffered in some countries where the very word 'city' raises the spectre of overcrowded slums, noise, disease, crime, and a lack of educational and recreational facilities. It is our determination that Canadian cities be healthy centres of human activity.

Membership in a community, Mr Speaker, imposes – and properly – certain limitations on the activities of all members. For this reason, while not lowering our guard or abandoning our proper interests, Canada must not appear to live by a double standard. We cannot, at the same time that we are urging other countries to adhere to régimes designed for the orderly conduct of international activities, pursue policies inconsistent with that order simply because to do so in a given instance appears to be to our brief advantage. Law, be it municipal or international, is composed of restraints. If wisely construed they contribute to the freedom and the well-being of individuals and of states. Neither states nor individuals should feel free to pick and choose, to accept or reject, the laws that may for the moment be attractive to them.

It is in this mood that the government is studying its claims to the waters lying off the islands of the Arctic archipelago. To close off those waters and to deny passage to all foreign vessels in the name of Canadian sovereignty, as some commentators have suggested, would be as senseless as placing barriers across the entrances to Halifax and Vancouver harbours. We should certainly prove by those acts that we were masters in our own house, but at immense cost economically by denying shipping of importance to Canada. On the other hand, if we were to act in some misguided spirit of international philanthropy by declaring that all comers were welcome without let or hindrance, we would be acting in default of Canada's obligations not just to Canadians but to all the world.

In the Canadian Arctic are found the breeding grounds, sometimes the only breeding grounds, of many species of migratory birds. Bylot Island is the nesting ground of the total population of the Greater Snow Goose. It is the site as well of the nesting colonies of some 6 million sea birds. Along 12 miles of the coast of Somerset Island are the nesting grounds of 4 million birds. Large numbers of air-breathing mammals – whales, seals, walrus – inhabit the waters lying throughout the Canadian archipelago. The existence of these and other animals and birds is dependent upon an uncontaminated environment; an environment which only Canada can take the lead in protecting. The beneficiaries of this natural life are not only Canadians; they are all the peoples of the world.

For those reasons, I say in this place, Mr Speaker, that Canada regards herself as trustee to all mankind for the peculiar ecological balance that now exists so precariously in the water, ice and land areas of the Arctic archipelago. We do not doubt for a moment that the rest of the world would find us at fault, and hold us liable, should we fail to ensure adequate protection of that environment from pollution or artificial deterioration. Canada will not permit this to happen, Mr Speaker. It will not permit this to happen either in the name of freedom of the seas, or in the interests of economic development. We have viewed with dismay the abuse elsewhere of both these laudable principles and are determined not to bow in the Arctic to the pressures of any state. In saying this, we are aware of the difficulties faced in the past by other countries in controlling water pollution and marine destruction within their own jurisdictions.

Part of the heritage of this country, a part that is of increasing importance and value to us, is the purity of our water, the freshness of our air, and the extent of our living resources. For ourselves and for the world we must jealously guard these benefits. To do so is not chauvinism; it is an act of sanity in an increasingly irresponsible world. Canada will propose a policy of use of the Arctic waters which will be designed for environmental preservation, Mr Speaker. This will not be an interference with the activities of others; it will not be a restriction upon progress. This legislation we regard, and invite the world to regard, as a contribution to the long-term and sustained development of resources for economic and social progress. We also invite the international community to join with us and support our initiative for a new concept, an international legal régime designed to ensure to human beings the right to live in a wholesome natural environment. In pursuit of this concept I shall be holding discussions shortly about this and other matters with the Secretary General of the United Nations. A combination of an international régime and the exercise by the Canadian government of its own authority in the Canadian Arctic will go some considerable distance to ensure that irreparable harm will not occur as a result of negligent or intentional conduct.

The same technology that has produced miracles of communication and transportation, of advances in the application of all the sciences ... remains as the most formidable opponent to a wholesome biosphere. We can no longer retreat from the health hazards which are the consequence of imperfect disposal of industrial and human wastes and from the incomplete combustion of fossil fuels. There is in nature a fantastic capacity for adaptation and regeneration, but it is not limitless. In the course of evolution, most species of life have disappeared because of their own, or their environment's, failure to cope with challenge to their survival. The adaptive processes of biological growth have simply not operated rapidly enough to

meet the challenges in time. Man's ingenuity and pre-emi-
nence, however, create an illusion of invulnerability to these
natural laws. Yet there is no reason to exempt man from the
possibility of extinction. All too often he has used his ingenuity and his capabilities not to meet the challenges he faces, but
instead to challenge his own survival. In doing so he threatens
not only himself but as well all species of life on this planet.

This government is determined, Mr Speaker, that, in Canada at least, these acts of folly will not be permitted to continue unchecked and uncontrolled.

House of Commons, 24 October 1969

If part of our heritage is our wilderness, and if the measure of
Canada is the quality of the life available to Canadians, then
we must act should there by any threat to either. We must act
to protect the freshness of our air and the purity of our water;
we must act to conserve our living resources. If necessary, we
must offer leadership to the world in these respects and with-
stand the cries of complaining vested interests.

The Arctic ice pack has been described as the most significant
surface area of the globe, for it controls the temperature of
much of the Northern Hemisphere. Its continued existence in
unspoiled form is vital to all mankind. The single most imminent threat to the Arctic at this time is that of a large oil spill.
Not only are the hazards of Arctic navigation much greater
than are found elsewhere, making the risk of break-up or sinking one of constant concern , but any major maritime tragedy
there would have disastrous and irreversible consequences.

The deleterious effects to the environment of a major oil spill
would be so much greater than those of a spill of similar size
in temperate or tropical waters that the result can be said with
scientific accuracy to be qualitatively different. For example,
the injuries which could result cannot be measured in terms of
dollars, as they can elsewhere, because the damages would not
be of a temporary nature. Nor is there now known any technique or process which can control, dispel or reduce vagrant
oil loose in Arctic waters. Such oil would spread immediately

beneath ice many feet thick; it would congeal and block the breathing holes of the peculiar species of mammals that frequent the region; it would destroy effectively the primary source of food for Eskimos and carnivorous wildlife throughout an area of thousands of square miles; it would foul and destroy the only known nesting areas of several species of wild birds.

Because of the minute rate of hydrocarbon decomposition in frigid areas, the presence of any such oil must be regarded as permanent. The disastrous consequences which the presence would have upon the marine plankton, upon the process of oxygenation in Arctic North America, and upon other natural and vital processes of the biosphere, are incalculable in their extent.

Involved here, in short, are issues which even the more conservative of environmental scientists do not hesitate to describe as being of a magnitude which is capable of affecting the quality, and perhaps the continued existence, of human and animal life in vast regions of North America and elsewhere. These are issues of such immense importance that they demand prompt and effective action. But this huge area cannot be protected by Canada alone. Just as the Arctic environment is of benefit to many nations, so only, in the long run, will international controls be able effectively to protect it.

The biosphere is not divided into national compartments, to be policed and protected by national regulations. Yet neither is the current state of international law sufficiently developed to permit instant and effective protection for the Canadian Arctic against activities which are already underway. Our pollution legislation is without question at the outer limits of international law. We are pressing against the frontier in an effort to assist in the development of principles for the protection of every human being on this planet.

I look upon this [Arctic] pollution legislation to be as exciting and as imaginative a concept as this Government has as yet undertaken. If government activities can be associated with youth and with spring, then this one is. It is not jingoist; it is not anti-American. It is positive and it is forward-looking.

Canada has been told that this pollution legislation is unacceptable because it is allegedly inconsistent with long-standing principles of freedom of navigation. Those who say this evidently regard the climatic conditions of the Arctic as somehow similar to those close to the equator. This parallel we reject. Notwithstanding that map makers may choose to illustrate the areas between the islands of the Canadian Arctic archipelago in the same fashion as they denote the water areas in tropical archipelagos, the physical circumstances *in situ* are quite disparate. Most of the Arctic channels are covered with heavy thicknesses of ice during most months of the year. This ice has presented such a barrier to navigation through the centuries that there has not yet occurred a single commercial voyage through the Northwest Passage. Only through abstract theorization can the Northwest Passage be described as an 'international strait'. Only by an examination conceptually removed from reality can Beaufort Sea be described as 'high sea'.

I suggest that it is a disservice to the development of international law to argue that important principles should be applied in circumstances which are clearly inappropriate. The law of the sea has evolved over many years, and is now to a large degree codified. Canada has taken a leading and constructive role in this process. During this lengthy evolution, however, states have never contemplated waters that are other than fluid. Only a handful of special regulations have been developed to meet special ice situations. It is our view that at the present time there is no customary law applicable to navigation in Arctic areas, and that we cannot wait for a disaster to prompt us to act. We need law now to protect coastal states from the excesses of the shipping states.

Both as a stimulus to this necessary development and as a protection to all North Americans, we remain convinced that we must act immediately to legislate preventive measures for control of pollution, and we are doing so.

We have told our friends and neighbours that this Canadian step, designed to protect the Arctic waters, will not lead to anarchy; it is not a step which diminishes the international rule of law; it is not a step taken in disregard of the aspirations and interests of other members of the international community. Canadian action is instead an assertion of the importance of the environment, of the sanctity of life on this planet, of the need for the recognition of a principle of clean seas, which is in all respects as vital a principle for the world of today and tomorrow as was the principle of free seas for the world of yesterday.

For three hundred years, governments have devoted themselves to the increase of state wealth: through expansion of trade, through growth of the industrial base, through welfare programs to aid and re-train the victims of society. We have conducted these worthy activities in the belief that this planet is possessed of an inexhaustible supply of fresh air and clean water; a permanent balance of flora and fauna; an optimism born of the knowledge that nature is a force so strong it cannot be upset permanently.

We now know that this is not so. We now know that spring is not automatic. We now know that the responsibility is ours to restore and maintain the health of the biosphere. Without sunshine, without health, growth and wealth are meaningless. Every human being realizes this, but perhaps it is for Canada – the land of space, of youth, of spring – to take the lead, to depart from the insane course on which mankind has embarked and to return to the point where we and our children can say without hesitation ' God's in His Heaven, all's right with the world'.

Annual Meeting, Canadian Press, Toronto, 15 April 1970

There is no single source of pollution. In Canada, paper mills have been releasing mercury into fresh-water streams, chemical plants have been discharging phosphorus wastes, towns and cities have poured raw sewage into rivers. Perhaps more pervasively than any other cause, however, the production, transportation and use of fossil fuels – particularly petroleum – is destroying the life support system of many parts of the world. The fantastic quantities of oil that have gushed from the sea-bed into the Santa Barbara channel and into the Gulf of Mexico cannot be described adequately by the euphemistic word 'leak'. The break-up and sinking of oil tankers such as the *Torrey Canyon* off England, or the *Arrow* off Nova Scotia, make ludicrous the word 'spill'. These are monumental disasters. The fear of such an incident occurring in the unique geographic and climatic circumstances of the Canadian Arctic has led the Canadian government recently to propose legislation embodying new concepts for the protection of the delicate ecological balance found in the Arctic.

If governments do not prevent repetitions of this sort of activity, we are all in peril. Oil, phosphate detergents, and effluents act to inhibit, over-extend or destroy the photosynthetic production of oxygen in the oceans. The issue is not simply one of littering, or of offensive smells, as some industrialists would have us believe. The issue is one of life itself.

Perhaps the responsibility for acting decisively in this area should fall with greatest force upon countries such as ours, which are gifted with almost limitless space. We have, after all, the most to gain. As we come to appreciate the great value of our wilderness, so should we take whatever steps are necessary to preserve it. If we do not tackle systematically and effectively this simple problem – one which requires little more than determination and discipline – how can we suggest to some of our neighbours in this global village that they attack with more fortitude another of the great problems which threatens to stifle us, that of over-population? No complicated factors of religion, or culture, or lack of understanding compound our problem. Only greed and indifference stand in the way of a solution.

Wilderness forces men to be self-reliant, to be aware of their own failings and tolerant of the shortcomings of others. In the wilderness, horizons are broad and men are able to look ahead great distances. It is the frontier that tests the integrity of men, yet permits them to dream and to plan – as if the space about them expands their own consciousness. Kids who blow their minds on drugs are missing a much better – and much cheaper – thing: a trip into the Arctic, or into the outback. It's habit-forming, a habit that can't easily be kicked. It's high and it's wild. It's what turned on several generations of Australians and Canadians long before the age of chemicals. And it can still turn us on if we don't let our urban hang-ups drive us to despair. To blow out pollution and monotony, I urge everyone to take such a trip if at all possible. It will help them find themselves. And it will help young Canadians and Australians to find again the spirit of their own countries.

National Press Club, Canberra, Australia, 18 May 1970

My own opinion [on marijuana]?

Well, if you want my own opinion not as a legislator but as an individual I don't dig it. I respect the freedom of other people to do many of the things they want to do but it's not really ... My own opinion is that it's a form of getting high, perhaps not all that different from alcohol, not all that different from other forms of intoxication. I just personally don't believe in intoxication. I think it's a form of escape, it's a form of seeking your excitement or your release from the outside, from artificial means, whether it be alcohol, whether it be marijuana, whether it be hash, whether it be the harder stuff; and people who want to get high before going to a party, or take two or three cocktails in order to screw up enough courage to sit down to a big dinner, it's their choice. But it's not mine, if you're asking my opinion. I think especially when you're young, well, I wouldn't think much of a kid who had to take a shot of whiskey every other day in order to screw up his courage to go to school or do his homework. When you're old and forty like me, or more, you may look for artificial means of facing life and creating artificial paradises for yourself. But, once again, you're asking my own opinion, when you're young and fifteen and twenty, hell, there's so many exciting things to do in the world that you should try and get it from within you, and from the scenery or the events in the outside world, from music, from travelling, from everything rather than, once again, putting chemicals into your body whether it be drugs or whether it be smoke, or alcohol for that matter. You want my opinion – there it is.

Perhaps I shouldn't go on on this, but people who do it, I don't judge them any more than I judge a person who takes

At Igloolik, NWT, March 1970

alcohol. You know, it's their own health, but the same people who get high on pot five or three times a week very often are the same people who say, 'What's the government going to do about pollution?' and who go around polluting their own lungs.

Youth meeting, Whitehorse, Yukon, 4 August 1970

How many members of this House, I wonder, Mr Speaker, have walked through the main entrance of this building over the years either accepting without question, or failing to notice, the words carved in the stone above the doorway? How many today could agree with the language employed there? The inscription reads: 'The wholesome sea is at her gates: her gates both East and West'.

Wholesome though those seas may have been when the sculptor was at work, the excesses of shipowners and operators, combined over the years with the complacency of public and government, have led to foul water, unfit in places for any but the lowest forms of life.

These are the kinds of changes that must be resisted. Today, when we look to the seas at our gates, we gaze not in two but in three directions. Our third, northern sea must not be permitted to lose its present wholesome state, and to that end legislation was introduced into this House last session. Honourable members on all sides accepted the necessity for and the wisdom of this legislation and passed it through the House in a rare display of unanimity. I am grateful to them for doing so. Steps are now necessary to contain and remove the conditions of pollution on our western and eastern gates, and legislation to that end will soon be introduced. The battle against pollution elsewhere than in our coastal waters is to be waged with increasing vigour and efficiency.

House of Commons, 9 October 1970

Pollution is *not* a necessary by-product of industrialization. Pollution *is* a matter of concern for all countries. On this planet we all share, there is an absolute limit to the available quality of fresh water, pure air and the necessary elements for the recycling of oxygen. Should those qualities be overtaxed, either by the greed of thoughtless developed nations or by the ignorance of ambitious developing nations, the human race will be the loser. Without an understanding of this problem – and the assignment to its solution of the highest priority – all our development programs will be for naught. We shall find that in our common quest for a better life we shall have poisoned the very biosphere upon which we depend for life.

Prime Minister Gandhi's luncheon, New Delhi, India, 12 January 1971

Canadians, as much as any other persons in the world, are the products of our environment. We inhabit for the most part a narrow belt stretched across seven time zones, in a climate which varies from temperate to harsh to impossible. We learned long ago that it was necessary to live with our geography and our climate on nature's terms. No Canadian pioneer was so brash as to say that his aim was to compete with nature and conquer it. The pioneers knew it was necessary to live in harmony with nature. Few in this country have found resources in such abundance that they have not known the need for conservation.

Yet, suddenly, in the past two decades, the rush of technology has become so swift, the siren song of material gain so seductive, that we have permitted commercial processes to commence which we do not always understand, which may lead to disastrous consequences, and which may have cumulative effects. The word 'thalidomide' should forever be a warning to us. So should the phenomenon of DDT accumulation through the life cycles of maritime creatures. While I was in New Zealand last year, I was told by scientists of their findings of DDT in the fat of Antarctic penguins, more than 1,500 miles distant from the nearest inhabited land. In the name of economic growth, in the pursuit of comfort and pleasure, we have increased the demands upon our environment and posed new risks and new costs which are often far in excess of the value of the growth or the benefit of the comfort.

Technological accomplishment and population growth have both reached such a rate of acceleration that the world at this moment is placed precariously at the commencement of several exponential curves. Going up at a perilous pace are population and pollution; coming down at a rate deserving of equal concern are reserves of natural resources and acreage suitable for cultivation. We have been deluding ourselves for a quarter of a century with a misleading book-keeping system that permits industry, government, agriculture – every segment of the community – to pass on certain costs to society at large. No businessman would calculate his net gain without first taking into effect the deterioration of his plant building, the depreciation of his machinery, and the depletion of his stock of raw materials. Why then do western governments continue to worship at the temple of Gross National Product? Isn't it time we paid heed to resource exhaustion, to environmental deterioration, to the social costs of over-crowding, to the extent of solid waste disposal? Shouldn't we, in short, be replacing our reliance on GNP with a more revealing figure – a new statistic which might be called Net Human Benefit?

I do not deny that some government policies appear contradictory any more than it can be denied that society as a whole harbours contradictions. A community which will not tolerate a government decision to close a polluting plant, causing hundreds of persons to lose their jobs, will not hesitate for a moment to condemn the same government for its failure to protect the ecology.

Liberal Party of Vancouver, 1 May 1971

The north is one of the few frontiers remaining on this planet. It appears to us in Canada, as it does to you in the USSR, as a great challenge. Yet this challenge is accompanied by responsibilities, for in these Arctic areas is found the irony of strong, dedicated men and a fragile, often permafrost environment. The men, in their dedication, are capable of destroying the fragility of their surroundings. In our haste, therefore, to develop the north we must take care not to set in train events which will disturb the delicate ecological balance. We must ensure that this great environment is not scarred and polluted by man and machine.

Reply to Toast, Murmansk, USSR, May 1971

The World about Us

A peaceful world

Never before in history has the disparity between the rich and the poor, the comfortable and the starving, been so extreme; never before have mass communications so vividly informed the sufferers of the extent of their misery; never before have the privileged societies possessed weapons so powerful that their employment in the defence of privilege would destroy the haves and the have-nots indiscriminately. We are faced with an overwhelming challenge. In meeting it, the world must be our constituency.

Assistance [may be] in any form that will create the political, economic and human climate most conducive to the nurturing of human dignity. International activities of this breadth are a far cry from the earlier and more primitive concepts of direct financial assistance. In their impact and in their value, they are also a long way from charity and philanthropy. If the Canadian goal is to assist other states in this way, then we are involved with humanity. And we are involved for our mutual benefit.

I emphasize this because when one benefits from an activity one is less likely to object to its cost. How do we benefit? In several respects:
a. A world community of nations freely co-operating should result in a lessening of international tension. This would lead to a world less susceptible to war. Canada and Canadians

At Fortune, Nfld., August 1971

would become more secure, and in this troubled world, that would be benefit beyond measure.

b. A multiplicity of nations possessing expanding economies would mean that standards of living would rise and world markets would multiply. Canadian products would find more purchasers, and for a trading nation such as Canada, that would be a benefit of great value.

c. In times of peace, men have turned their attention towards the development of their cultures, and the enrichment of life. Canadians live more meaningfully by enjoying the works of artists and scholars of whatever national source, and that is a benefit of unquestioned value.

These interests and these benefits submit to no national boundaries. The social, economic, and political betterment of any man anywhere is ultimately reflected in this country. If at the same time our consciences – our humanitarian instincts – are served, as they are and as they should be, then so much the better. Unquestionably the concept of international assistance is appealing because it is one of the most uplifting endeavours in which man has ever engaged. But we must never forget that in this process Canadians are beneficiaries as well as benefactors.

As Canadians we must realize that international co-operation, particularly in the field of economic assistance, in order to remain effective, must take on a new form. From the present pattern of commodity and food assistance, of gifts of manufactured goods and loans of money, we must, in response to the economic needs of the developing countries, turn more and more to preferential trade arrangements. The two United Nations Conferences on Trade and Development have made clear that economic aid, in order to be effective, must increasingly take the form of trade. ...

This kind of aid, these preferential trade arrangements, have no glamour attached to them. They cannot be illustrated by stirring photographs of rugged Canadian engineers posing before massive dams in remote places. This kind of aid doesn't offer a ready market to Canadian manufacturers, nor does it reduce our base metal or other commodity surpluses. In short, this kind of aid is competition, and bears little evidence of the sweet philanthropy which we have sometimes employed in the past to coat the cost of our aid 'pill'. Unless Canadians are aware of the vital goal our aid is seeking to achieve, they may not be sympathetic to a change of this sort. It is my opinion that Canadians will understand, and will accept the challenge. Economic aid, unless effective, will be useless. In order to be effective it will, in all likelihood, be costly. Yet we and the other developed nations have no alternative. The world cannot continue to accommodate mutually exclusive blocs of rich nations and poor nations.

We must recognize that, in the long run, the overwhelming threat to Canada will not come from foreign investments, or foreign ideologies, or even – with good fortune – foreign nuclear weapons. It will come instead from the two thirds of the peoples of the world who are steadily falling farther and farther behind in their search for a decent standard of living. This is the meaning of the revolution of rising expectations. I repeat, this problem is not new. But its very size, involving some two and a half billion people, makes it qualitatively different from what it has been in the past. Nevertheless, the observation of Chateaubriand, writing of a similar, but infinitely smaller problem in Europe a century and a half ago is worthy of repetition today. He stated:

'Try to convince the poor man, once he has learned to read and ceased to believe, once he has become as well informed as yourself, try to convince him that he must submit to every sort of privation, while his neighbour possesses a thousand times what he needs; in the last result you would have to kill him.'
University of Alberta, Edmonton, 13 May 1968

Our primary responsibility, Mr Speaker, is to the people of Canada, but the efforts of Parliament to produce a better life must not be confined for the benefit solely of Canadians. In comparison with the daily lives of the great majority of humanity, Canadians are immensely fortunate – whether measured in terms of political rights, in terms of freedom from the fear of violence or in terms of standard of living. By contrast, two thirds of mankind live in a state of perpetual misery and struggle, with per capita annual incomes measured in hundreds, not thousands, of dollars. The world is now too small to permit such disparities to continue. Unless these differences are eliminated, the pressures on the rich nations will become so intense as to force them either to share in equal measure or to make decisions of frightenting moral consequence. By the year 2000, the population of the world will be 7.5 billion – twice what it is today; 80 per cent of these people will be living in the developing countries. There is no rational or moral justification for a lack of response now by Canada and other developed nations to their undeniable needs ...

These are sobering and frightening thoughts. They explain the decision of Canada, at this time of austerity in most governmental programmes, to increase the value of our foreign economic assistance budget, and to create, after extensive planning and consultation with other countries, an International Development Research Centre which will be charged with the responsibility of improving the qualitative effect of Canadian and other aid projects. The Centre is an exciting concept – a recognition that accelerated economic growth is a complex task – and is deeply interrelated with problems of social development. I am sure that all honourable members will agree that it is fitting that Canada, long among the most active of contributors to foreign aid – and this year the host to the twentieth annual meeting of the Colombo Plan countries – should take a lead in this important respect. It must continue to be the responsibility of all of us here to ensure that Canadians will understand the need, and support increasing expenditures, for developmental programmes.

House of Commons, 24 October 1969

There are mysteries in this land, Mr Prime Minister, mysteries of nature and of God which are beyond the comprehension of human beings: the instinct which directs giant sea turtles to return from the depths of the ocean, in order to lay their eggs on the beaches of Kelantan; the ability of the Temiar to resolve tendencies of violence through nocturnal dreams. These mysteries cause men to be humble. They should also cause man to recognize that this planet on which he lives is not his to use as he pleases – to deface or to destroy; that he dwells here subject to certain immutable laws which he breaks only at his peril. Man's restless energy is capable of destroying himself and the very world into which he was born, or it may serve to overcome the liabilities of disease and starvation which have visited him since the beginning of time, and permit man to pursue a joyous life.

The choice is man's to make. No new scientific discovery is needed; no new source of revenue is required. All man needs to do in order to enjoy a life of richness and satisfaction in a world full of beauty and opportunity is to accept as his brother all other human beings.

State Dinner, Kuala Lumpur, Malaysia, May 1970

It is a wise man who realizes how shallow and how narrow is his understanding of others. In one man's lifetime he may come to know deeply only a few persons, may come to understand with great confidence only a few ideas. For a monk in a monastery – perhaps even for the scholar of three centuries ago – those limitations caused no insurmountable problems. Better that a man know little and know it well than to know much and not understand it.

But in this year 1970 the two immutable ingredients of life, which have been available without distinction to all men in all places throughout history, are no longer with us. No more may we shield ourselves with either time or distance. In the age of satellite communications systems and intercontinental ballistic missiles, the transmission of information and the transmission of lethal destructive power are both virtually instantaneous. Yet skilful as we are in propelling messages and bombs, we remain in the dark ages in our attempts to communicate understanding.

If man has learned nothing else in the past quarter of a century, he has surely come to know of the interdependence on this shrunken planet of all persons and all nations. If he has not learned that, then nothing can save us from the inevitable destructive effects of our own greed and shortsightedness.

I believe that we shall profit from this knowledge and that we shall make the necessary accommodations. Events of the magnitude of Expo 67 and Expo 70 serve to illustrate in dramatic fashion the richness of man's culture, the unlimited

capabilities of his mental powers, and the basic happiness of his nature. These are qualities of immense value – we should understand them, treasure them, and rejoice in them.
State Dinner, Tokyo, Japan, May 1970

A Canadian at Osaka realizes with some shock just how deeply his background, his upbringing and his education have conditioned him, when looking at the world, to gaze first – almost subconsciously – towards Europe. To a Canadian in the 1970s, Asia should not be thought of as the Far East. Japan is east of Canada only if it is approached by the long route – long in terms of distance, and long in terms of history. It is time now to take the direct route, the route of the closing decades of the century. I would like to think that our current visit to Canada's Pacific neighbours and our presence here today will signal a new beginning. Canadians should view the far side of the Pacific on its own terms, not through the eyes of European events or of European historians. We should recognize that Canadians and Japanese are located on the opposite sides of a single ocean. As a result of Canadian participation at Expo 70, Japan and the Pacific countries in Asia shall be referred to by Canadians, I hope, not as 'the Far East', but as 'our New West'.

If we do so, we will find that we will have learned something of considerable value in the brief interval since Expo 67: we will have learned more about Man and His World than our forefathers were permitted to learn over a period of many decades. And we will show as well that we are ready to learn a great deal more from Expo 70. For only by understanding where we stand on this global home will we be able to plan with confidence a future of progress and harmony for mankind.
Canada Day, Expo 70, Osaka, Japan, May 1970

If it is possible to marry the ageless understanding of the East with the application of modern technology from the West, as I believe it is, then it may well be in India that the espousal will occur. Even if we in the West possessed no other motivation for our economic assistance programs, the repayment of the immense legacy of wisdom, of art, of philosophy, of knowledge – those elements that distinguish the civilized man from the savage – would by itself be more than sufficient reason to do what we can to share with you those skills with which we have been favoured by geography and circumstance. The immensity of the challenge – co-operation in raising the economic base of the second most populous nation in the world – should no more deter us in our endeavour than did the immensity of the task which faced your philosophers and teachers deter them in the pursuit of their goals. The material poverty of India in the twentieth century is nothing as compared with the spiritual and artistic poverty of much of the world in centuries past.

Prime Minister Gandhi's luncheon, New Delhi, India
12 January 1971

Your society long ago accomplished what western countries are only now coming to understand – that man's immediate environment is more than a background for his life; it is reflected into his very being and exercises an influence on his moods and his attitudes.

How fortunate Indonesians are in the richness of their artistic heritage! Access to art and drama is available not just to the rich or to the privileged but to every village dweller. Is there anywhere in the world where millions of women dress in fabrics which are not simply cloth but are in many cases batik, works of art? Where else in the world do such numbers of people have the opportunity to participate in such marvellous drama and fantasy as is offered by a *wayang* shadow play? What other country includes within its bounds an island such as Bali where every resident is an artist of some sort – painter, dancer, sculptor, musician? In Bali, indeed in Indonesia, folk art is not so much an individual accomplishment as it is a social manifestation.

State Dinner, Jakarta, Indonesia, 22 January 1971

This is an historic occasion for Canada, the first visit by a Canadian Prime Minister to one of the world's great powers; an occasion which represents many years of painstaking work by our two governments in laying the groundwork for a constructive working relationship between our countries.

It represents as well, I hope, the beginning of a new period in which we will find ourselves able to do more together.

It is altogether appropriate that we should co-operate. The Soviet Union and Canada are, after all, near neighbours, even though it is only in recent years that this fact has been understood widely. The vast Arctic wastes have formed historically such a prohibitive barrier to all forms of surface travel that our two countries appeared on maps and in the minds of most people as being very distant one from the other. Only in recent years have we come to realize that we are geographically contiguous.

It has taken space satellites in orbit, and long-range aircraft flying great circle routes, to bring home to us that your country, Mr Chairman, and mine, occupy the opposite shores of a single ocean. This recent perspective – a top-of-the-world perspective – has made each of us aware as well of the immense proportion of the other's country that lies within an Arctic or sub-Arctic latitude. Canada and the Soviet Union are without question the two largest Arctic states in the world. We have in common many problems, many challenges, and many responsibilities.

The problems are those posed by bitter climates, immense distances, and difficult terrain. The challenges are found in the resources which await discovery, the transportation required for their development, and the provision of shelter and services for the people living and working in the north. The responsibilities are to all mankind – to protect the delicate ecological balance of the Arctic, to prevent the pollution of the Arctic Ocean, to husband and conserve the unique biological resources of that part of the globe.

The Soviet Union and Canada have, of course, many more reasons than the Arctic to be interested in one another. Our geographic positions give to each of us a rather special perspective on the world; an understanding of space and distance which I believe permits us to look beyond the differences of our social and political systems and seek actively those advantages which can be derived from a world in which tensions are lowered and the energies of men are devoted totally to positive goals. Our perspective in this respect is assisted by a further dimension, one which is a product of the many races and cultures which make up the population of our two countries. We in Canada and you in the Soviet Union benefit from this enriching process and, in the result, look upon the world from an understanding point of view.

This is the first occasion on which my wife has been to Russia, yet she has sensed already the timeless appeal of this old but new nation. I carry with me fond memories of my previous visits to your country – of the quiet mood of the great city of Moscow beneath a blanket of fresh snow, of the joy of a feast in Georgia, of the strength of the love which the Russian people hold for their land. I thought when here before of the lovely words of Konstantin Simonov. He wrote:

> Just wait for me and I'll return ...

I have returned. Not this time as a private citizen but in some ways as a guide for all those Canadians who have not visited the Soviet Union but who will learn much about it in the next few days through the pens and the cameras of the journalists who have accompanied me.

Response to toast of Premier Alexei Kosygin, Kremlin luncheon May 1971

Perhaps because of Christopher Marlowe, many westerners tend to think of Samarkand only as the city of Tamurlane. It is good to be reminded, however, that Samarkand then, like the Tashkent of today, was even more the creation of its great builders and workmen. In the perspective of human development, we should perhaps place highest the names of such great Samarkand poets as Jami and Navoi, and the scholar Ulug-Beg, who recalculated here the positions of a thousand stars less eight.

Some of the greatest contributions to human progress have been made by scientists and scholars, not warriors or politicians. Few people today can recall who was Prime Minister of Great Britain in the time of Isaac Newton, or who ruled Sicily in the time of Archimedes. It is interesting to speculate the names which will be remembered from our time in the centuries to come. Perhaps there are artists or scientists working here in this city right now who will have earned their niche in eternity. It would be well if this could be so; for the power of men to destroy has never been so great as it is today, or the opportunities for creative geniuses to exercise a positive influence so vast. Like the sorcerer's apprentice, we must learn to curb the desire to try out all the wonder-working gadgets which technology has placed in our grasp. A sober and thorough effort must be made by all men in authority to achieve a deep and honest understanding of this world, to husband and divide wisely its resources, in order that it may be preserved and enhanced for the benefit of future generations.

Just as in your cities of Samarkand and Tashkent we can see the treasures of the past preserved while the cities of the future take shape around them, so on a world scale, we must preserve the valuable treasures and traditions of the past while we build for the future. In the shrinking world of today this necessitates strong international co-operation to determine and to share the resources of the earth: its air, its waters, its fish, and even the use of the heavenly spaces that surround it.
Reply to toast, Tashkent, USSR, May 1971

What you have accomplished here under inhibiting conditions of geography, climate and permafrost is surely one of the modern marvels of the world – and one which sets a standard in Arctic living for all other countries. My introduction to Norilsk is all the more dramatic because we have flown here directly from Tashkent, 2,000 miles to the south and 40 degrees centigrade warmer. Only one other country in the world is so vast that a person is able to travel such a distance in a north-south direction and still have room left over within its borders. That country is Canada. This spaciousness and sense of immense distances has left a very real impression on the character of Canada and Canadians, as I am sure it has on citizens of the Soviet Union. For that reason alone we have something in common one with another, and for the same reason we are distinct from those who live in smaller and more congested states.

We who live in far northern climes have something else in common – the experience of facing the challenge of a bitter climate over long periods, a challenge which disciplines men and women and forces them to look deep within themselves to find the stamina and resourcefulness necessary for survival and accomplishment. The fact of your survival here is self-evident; the level of your accomplishments ... as we have seen, is nothing short of spectacular.

Reply to toast, Norilsk, USSR, May 1971

As we have looked traditionally south to the United States and east to Europe and, more recently, west to Asia, so should we not disregard our neighbour to the north. The relations between Canada and the Soviet Union in the post-war years have not all been of a wholesome or a desirable nature. I harbour no naive belief that as a result of this protocol our two countries will find themselves suddenly in a relationship which will reflect nothing but sweetness and tender feelings. As I stated in my speech in the Kremlin, there remain many fundamental differences between us; differences relating to deep-seated concerns springing from historic, geographic, ideological, economic, social and military factors.

But surely, Mr Speaker, the only way to resolve these differences and eliminate these concerns is by increased contact and effort at understanding. That is what the protocol proposes. That is what, in a different way, is achieved by prime ministerial visits. Through them an opportunity is created by the pens of journalists and the cameras of photographers for the people of both Canada and the Soviet Union to learn much more about one another – their respective histories, their sufferings, their aspirations.

No one can travel in the Ukraine and not absorb the instinctive and passionate desire for peace on the part of a people who lost nine million of their countrymen during World War II, a number approaching in magnitude the entire population of Canada at that time. No one can walk through the cemeteries of Leningrad and view the mass graves of tens of thousands of residents of that city who died of starvation during the cruel 900-day siege and not understand that the

At a sugaring-off party, St Joseph-du-Lac, March 1971

Russian people fear desperately the repetition of an experience which no Canadians, fortunately, have ever suffered. The death of half the people of a city – 600,000 of them women, children and civilians – did not spare a single Leningrad family. The survivors of that cruel conflict do not regard war as an abstract concept, as a glorious pursuit or as a credible means of resolving disputes. War to them is the loss before one's eyes of loved ones, of home, of possessions, of hope.

To achieve a satisfactory, just and continuing peace requires a climate of confidence, a climate in which men of differing social and economic systems trust one another. There is no simple way in which this can be done, but neither is there the slightest doubt that it must be done. Equally, confidence can be engendered only by increasing contact of governments and of people. In this way, gradually, and sometimes painfully, can we continue and accelerate the slow progress toward a world in which the foremost goals of every government of every country must be the attainment of social justice, fundamental human rights and the dignity and worth of all human beings.

House of Commons, 28 May 1971

The first visit here of a premier of the Soviet Union ... is evidence of the positive work in which our two countries have been engaged for several years, work designed to emphasize the advantages to be gained from a constructive working relationship.

Most obvious of these advantages are the direct and immediate benefits that will flow to both our peoples, such as those from our exchanges in the scientific and technical fields.

Less obvious, but far more important, are the indirect benefits that will be reaped in the future: those that will be ours because we have come to know one another, and to understand one another. Knowledge is the basis of understanding. In understanding, and in that alone, lies the hope that men and women – different though they be in ideology, colour or creed – will be able to live together peacefully and advantageously.

I do not think I am overstating the case. We live in a small world, with great problems. Antagonisms fester in a climate of misunderstanding. Only when we know each other well can we be moved to build on what we have in common rather than to be frightened by our differences. Fright is one of the most insidious of human failings. It leads to distrust, suspicion and – eventually – hatred. In this nuclear age we cannot afford the luxury of hatred.

Friendship is not easily won. Like other valuables it is rare, and one must work to attain it. More than that, one must work to keep it. Both our countries, Mr Premier, are aware that true friendship, when once attained, and if soundly based, is strong enough to endure temporary differences, and to emerge stronger for having been tested. Canada's long relationship with its oldest friends is proof to us that, however uncertain may be the consequences from time to time of short-term events, the long run consists of a climate of understanding and co-operation.

It is my sincere hope, Mr Premier, indeed my confident belief, that Canada and the Soviet Union are now launched on a path that will permit the development of just such a relationship. Canada and Canadians want very much to be able to look to the north, as they long have looked to the south, and see friends in each direction.

Perhaps the first step toward understanding is a frank appraisal not only of the similarities which join us but also of the differences which now distinguish our policies. We perform no service to ourselves, Sir, or to one another, if we do not face reality. In this respect I should like to repeat some of the words I used on the occasion of the Soviet government lunch in the Kremlin last May. I said to you and your colleagues at that time: 'I do not wish to leave the impression that Canada and the Soviet Union have no differences. Nor do I minimize the breadth of some of those differences; they concern points of more than academic or legalistic interest. They relate to deep-seated concerns springing from historic, geographic, ideological, economic, social and military factors. Nevertheless, as governments, many of our objectives are similar. We seek for our peoples a world without war, a world in which governments are at the service of man – to raise the standard of living, to eliminate disease and want, to attempt to make life a happier experience. In respect of some of these goals, Soviet-Canadian co-operation and agreement may hurry their attainment. I hope that our discussions this week will germinate some helpful ideas. But ideas, like seeds, need soil to grow in, and in this case the soil is confidence. I believe that our discussions of bilateral problems can help to promote confidence, and so can our discussion of international problems'.

The move toward confidence made considerable progress last spring. Your visit here is another important step forward.

Toast to Premier Alexei Kosygin of USSR, *Canadian Government Dinner, Ottawa, 18 October 1971*

Foreign relations

In a very real sense civilization and culture in North America are more menaced, more strongly menaced, more strongly threatened, by internal disorders than by external pressure.

I feel very strongly that disorder in the great cities of the United States of America, problems created by urbanization, problems created by racial strife, problems created by unrest in many sectors of society – not only the young and the trade unions but also the new élites in the North American society – I believe these troubles may quite seriously lead to large rebellions and large disturbances of civil order and of social stability in North America.

And I believe that if in the next half a dozen years or so there were to be great riots and beginnings of civil war in the United States of America, I am quite certain they would overflow the borders and they would perhaps link up with the underprivileged Mexican and the underprivileged Canadian it might be the peon south of the American border but in Canada it might be the Indian, it might be the Métis, it might be a lot of underprivileged in Canada. I don't think it would be the separatists, but that is another argument. I personally happen to believe that these sources of disturbance are areas which we should fear and seek to correct with as great urgency as perhaps anything that is happening in Europe.

And for this reason I am very concerned that the Canadian government through its own policies, and through any influence it might have on its friends and allies in and out of

NATO, get people to understand this, that in a very real sense we are not so much threatened by the ideologies of Communism or of Fascism or even, I would say, so much threatened by atomic bombs and ICBMs, as we are by the very large sectors of the world – two-thirds of the world's population – that goes to bed hungry every night and large fractions of our own society which do not find fulfilment in this society.

And this is the background of these reviews [of foreign and defence policy] in which we are embarked. I am not predicting what the outcome will be, but I am saying that in my scale of values I am perhaps less worried now about what might happen over the Berlin Wall than what might happen in Chicago, New York, and perhaps our own great cities in Canada.

Question & Answer Session, Queen's University, Kingston, Ont., 8 November 1968

There is in Canada at the present time a growing sense of unease that in a nation as rich as ours there is a problem of widespread poverty; that among people as dispassionate and understanding as are Canadians there is linguistic apprehensiveness and inequality; that in a world possessed of the technological means to journey to the planets, there exist terrifying threats to our environment and to our very existence.

Canada, by itself, cannot solve all these problems and perhaps not even some of them. But we firmly believe that we can and must apply our talents and our resources in such a fashion as to seek solutions and, where appropriate, to persuade other states to co-operate with us in seeking these solutions. We have some qualifications for these tasks, and we have had considerable valuable experience which might prove to be of assistance to other states afflicted with similar problems. This is so partly because these qualifications, this experience, and the conditions which have spawned them, are similar in many respects to the differences and the difficulties which are found in the larger world community. And I wish to list some of them.

Canada is a federal state, the same as the USA. Yet, two of our provinces – Ontario and Quebec – are so populous in comparison with the other eight as to give to them an immensely influential position.

Nor is wealth in our country any more equitably distributed. The per capita income of the richest province is about twice that of the poorest, and we have elaborate arrangements for redistribution of tax revenues among the provinces of Canada.

Only one-third of all Canadians are of a stock that had English as its mother tongue, although two-thirds of the population live and work in English; the other third speak French daily as their normal means of communication – socially, in commerce and with government. Within Canada there are French-speaking universities, radio and television networks, newspapers and labour unions. There is a complete language community.

Another item: Our economy is founded largely upon foreign trade. In this respect I should pause to point out that we sell more to the United States, and buy more from the United States, than any other country in the world. The immense size of this trade bears out this emphasis. Canada's purchases from the United States each year exceed in value the total purchases of your four next largest trading partners (Japan, Britain, Germany, and France) combined – more than your total sales to all of Latin America.

So it is this pattern of uneven economic development, this heritage of linguistic diversity, and this dependence upon continued international intercourse that leads us to think that perhaps by way of some example we may be of benefit to a world which is so desperately seeking solutions to pressing problems.

As I say this, I hope that we Canadians do not have an exaggerated view of our own importance. We prefer to think that our place in the world is such that we can occasionally experiment with good ideas without risking a complete upset of the whole international order.

We are as pleased as is any country when our views are sought or our assistance requested. But we may be excused, I hope, if we fail to take too seriously the suggestion of some of our friends from time to time that our acts – or our failure to

act – this or that way will have profound international consequences or will lead to widescale undesirable results.
National Press Club, Washington, DC, *25 March 1969*

What the government is seeking in the review [of foreign and
defence policy] is something more than a catalogue of current
problems, useful though that would be. We are attempting to
learn whether Canada, by reassessing in a systematic fashion
its own and the world situation, may play a more effective role
in pursuing its objectives. We want to be sure that we are
doing, so far as we are able, the right things in the right
places. Canada's resources, both human and physical, are immense, but they are not limitless. We must establish priorities
which will permit us to expend our energies in a fashion that
will best further the values that we cherish.

We do not further those values by withdrawing from the
world, nor will this government ever suggest that we should.
But neither do we further those values effectively by need-
lessly fragmenting our efforts, by doing things that others can
and should do better. Above all, we accomplish nothing by refusing to recognize that in the past two decades there have
been changes in the world and in Canada which demand fresh
policies and adjusted viewpoints.

In some respect, Mr Speaker, it may be said that the foreign
policy review is a clinical test of Canada's maturity. The policies that are being examined were formulated and pursued
over a period of time that can only be described as an outstanding chapter in the history of this country. Canada's contribution to the betterment of international relations in the
post-war era is one of which all Canadians are justifiably
proud. But the record of that period reveals that Canada's efforts were successful largely because of our ability to innovate,
to meet new problems with new solutions, and to be aware
that the world is a constantly changing place.

The man whose name is associated with brilliant states-
manship by millions of people around the globe, the Canadian
who rightly earned for this country a proud place in the coun-
cils of the world, and was honoured with a Nobel Peace Prize,
did not achieve his success by adhering stubbornly to old poli-

cies. (Incidentally, Mr Speaker, the Right Honourable Lester B. Pearson is today celebrating his 72nd birthday in Tokyo where he is still exercising a service for the benefit of the world community.) Had Mr Pearson not approached new problems with new solutions, we would not regard him now with the respect he so richly deserves as a servant of peace.

And so it is today. Canadians must be prepared to face the world of actuality, the world of 1969.

We begin with the realization that we in Canada are in a relatively happy and unusual position. Not since Confederation has there existed a viable threat to our territorial integrity. The good fortune of geography has removed Canadian territory from physical contact with wars elsewhere; the good fortune of history has given us land frontiers with only a single, friendly nation. But we must remember that while there may be no present threat to Canada's territorial integrity, we are not able to say that there is no present threat from without to Canada's physical security. Should a major world conflict break out it will not likely involve territorial aggrandisement at Canada's expense, but it could easily involve mass destruction within Canada.

In a world as interdependent as that of today, with instant world-wide communications systems, and pre-targeted nuclear armed rockets only minutes flying time distant from all major European and North American cities, Canada's security is dependent on a peaceful world. Our efforts to achieve such a world are therefore a necessity; they should be made as effective as possible. Physical security now, and in the long run, can be secured only if the nations of the world recognize that certain conditions must obtain. I believe that there are five such conditons; in the long run the final three offer the only hope for lasting security.

1. Prevention of the erosion or serious imbalance of the nuclear arms stalemate which has so far been successful in deterring a nuclear holocaust;

2. Co-operation in preventing, or in promptly settling conflicts of a nature that might, by their location, escalate into nuclear war;

3. Participation in international peacekeeping forces and in non-military initiatives which will foster trust and strength in

international conflict-resolution procedures and in an effective system of world order;

4. Dedication of adequate resources to the study and negotiation of arms limitations and disarmament agreements;

5. Contribution of an increasing percentage of national resources to activities which are designed to relieve or remove such causes of unrest as economic insecurity.

These conditions must prevail in the international community if mankind is to survive the twentieth century. International mechanisms now exist to co-ordinate and further activities leading to these ends; they deserve and require the support of all governments, of men of all political leanings.

The Canadian government must consider which of these five conditions is deserving of the greatest expenditure at any given time, and toward which Canadian activity can be most effectively directed. Because none of the conditions can obtain through the efforts of any single nation, Canada's decisions in these matters must be taken after consultation with other states in the world community, but not necessarily with the same states in each instance.

In all history, arms by themselves have never guaranteed security for long. And just as there is no single cause of conflict, so is there no single technique of arms control. The present balance of deterrents is an absurdly unsatisfactory substitute for real security. A more stable alternative is necessary ...

It is the intention of this government that our foreign policy should provide for a growing investment of intellectual resources in this important area, and that one of the most important foreign relations tasks in which Canada is engaged is that which is directed to arms limitations and disarmament.
House of Commons, 23 April 1969

Q   Mr Prime Minister, the two leading Communist countries of the world, the Soviet Union and the People's Republic of China, have expressed cordiality toward your government and receptivity to your ideas. You have very close relations with the United States, fraternal relations with Britain and France and special relations with Japan. Two questions: What have the Communist countries to learn from you and what have you to learn from them? And the second question: Can we preserve our place inside the western alliance if you carry out the purpose of the protocol which you signed with the Soviet Union yesterday?

A   Well, on the first question, what the Soviet Union has to learn from Canada: here again I am not briefed to answer on their behalf. I am sure that in terms of trade, our past experience particularly thus far in the area of wheat but growingly in other areas, there has been some valid exchange. We signed last January an agreement on industrial application of science and technology which was entered into because, I presume, they felt that they had something to learn of Canadian technology. Beyond that, I am sure that they consider us an important member of the NATO alliance and that it is not of little interest to them to be able to talk to us directly and let us know their point of view on many questions.

But from our own point of view, it is quite clear that we have a great deal to learn from the Soviet Union. It is one of the two super-powers in the world today; one of the poles of influence, not only a military but an economic, technological, cultural pole of great significance and it is, moreover, Canada's neighbour across the Arctic Seas. It is a country from which we have a great deal to benefit in terms of exchanges in these areas I've mentioned, trade, culture, science, technology. But politically also, it is such a great and important country that it will be of great value to Canada to be able to have regular meetings and exchanges of points of view with the Soviet Union. As is well known, Canada is not only a good friend and neighbour of the United States of America, but also its ally in NATO and NORAD, and Canada has increasingly found it important to diversify its channels of communication because of the overpowering presence of the United States of America, and that is reflected in a growing consciousness amongst Canadians of the danger of our national identity from a cultural, economic and perhaps even military point of view. It has been the desire of the Canadian people and certainly reflected by this government to, I repeat, diversify our points of contact with the significant powers in the world. That is one of the reasons incidentally why we explained that we remained in NATO as we did because we found it useful to discuss a variety of subjects, not only with our close neighbour but also with our other friends and allies in NATO. And this reasoning applies even more strongly as regards the Soviet Union, which is not our ally in any alliance but which is one, I repeat, of the super-powers, and if they can take time to discuss with us various aspects of policy and various events in the world which might lead to threatening the peace, we are very glad for that and it will permit us to arrive at as independent an opinion on world events as we can possibly formulate.

The second part of your question I believe had to do with a question whether this protocol would in any way conflict with our belonging to NATO. Is that the essence of the question?

Q   Yes.

A   I don't see how it can.

Q   And NORAD?

A   Or NORAD. I don't see how it can. Both NATO and NORAD are military alliances though they have other aspects too, economic and cultural and political. But in no way do they preclude friendly relationships with other countries outside of NORAD or of NATO. On the contrary, it is quite obvious ... Well, there have been frequent contacts between Great Britain, France, Germany and the Soviet Union; the United States itself is discussing on a permanent basis now in the Strategic Arms Limitation Talks with the Soviet Union; West Germany has signed, less than a year ago, a treaty with the Soviet Union. I think there is nothing conflicting in all these acts and the fact that some of these countries and ourselves belong to NATO or NORAD. I think if we want to be informed participants in NORAD and in NATO, it is essential that Canada have its own points of view on European and other events. We have tried to do that in the past. You will recall that our decision regarding NATO two years ago was to reduce, as it were, any danger of Canadian participation in Europe being interpreted in a provocative sense and that is why we decided to phase out the nuclear role of our aircraft in NATO and so on. All these are indications that Canada within NATO has been pressing for a peaceful line and towards mutual and balanced force reductions and, I repeat, the more information we can have about the intentions of countries belonging to the Warsaw Pact, the more useful we will be.

Press Conference, Moscow, 20 May 1971

The foreign policy review stated that we would seek actively opportunities to further Canadian interests; that wherever possible we would not wait passively for events to occur and then to react to them; that, in short, we would pursue in as judicious and advantageous a way as possible the broad range of policies which are permitted to Canada as a country which is well respected abroad.

These things we have been doing, and these things we shall continue to do.

While in no way diluting our friendship or our contacts with those countries such as the United States, Britain, France and others with which we have had traditional and friendly relations, we have taken a fresh look at the world and at the Canadian interests in it. Areas of the world which have not in the past figured prominently in Canada have been sought out consciously as friends, as prospective trading partners, as sources of information and advice, as contributors to an independent Canada, a Canada not overwhelmingly dependent upon or dominated by any one state or group of states – in short, a Canada with a singular identity and well recognized as such both by Canadians and by citizens of other countries.

We have been active in the world in those areas where we could contribute positively and usefully: economic and technical assistance, through the creation of the Canadian International Development Research Centre; fresh juristic concepts for the prevention of pollution in waters off our shores and for the conservation of fisheries; studies and proposals in the fields of disarmament and arms control. We have looked to Latin America and are seeking permanent observer status in the Organization of American States; we have expressed our many-faceted interest in the countries of the far rim of the Pacific; we have adjusted our defence posture to remove from it any elements that could be regarded as provocative, and to ensure that our policy adequately but truly reflects the needs of Canada for national defence; we have been successful in establishing useful and official contacts with the most populous nation in the world, the People's Republic of China; we have entered wholeheartedly the new Francophonie organization

All this has been done, Mr Speaker, while retaining Canadian membership in NATO and NORAD, while strengthening our relationship with such economic associations as the OECD and GATT, while contributing in an effective and constructive fashion to the UN and to the Commonwealth.

These activities are good in themselves, are good for Canada and, I am convinced, are supported strongly by the majority of Canadians.

House of Commons, 28 May 1971

My fellow travellers and I were all greeted with warmth and friendliness when we were in Russia and I am confident that this attitude will find its way into a number of channels – permitting both effective inter-governmental relations and profitable commercial relations between our two countries. Patience and firmness will be required in order to penetrate the Soviet market, but the important thing is that the door is open. Just as it is now open to China, and has opened further recently in such countries as Indonesia.

In the past fortnight, a shipload of wood-pulp left the port of Vancouver bound for China – the first penetration into a market heretofore dominated by the Scandinavians. Had we not recognized the People's Republic of China, there is not the slightest doubt that that transaction, with all the potential it implies, would not have been completed. Two months ago, a Canadian bank commenced business in Indonesia – the first foreign bank to be permitted to do so in several years. Last week the Soviet government agreed to pay 235 million dollars into the Canadian economy in the next year and a half in return for an immense volume of wheat. Last week, too, the NATO foreign ministers, encouraged by Mitchell Sharp, agreed to welcome and encourage the invitation of Secretary General Brezhnev to engage in discussions leading to mutual and balanced force reduction – a natural extension of the Canadian-Soviet communiqué.

I think these are exciting developments. I think these bode well for a better world and a better Canada. As a trading nation, and as a people who have nothing to gain and much to lose from war, Canada and Canadians are better off in a world of tolerance and friendship. It is only common sense that our voice will be heard more clearly and more effectively in capitals with which we are on friendly terms – as the examples I have mentioned, and many more, clearly demonstrate.

The Conservative agriculture spokesman suggested last week that Russian wheat contracts aren't worth the paper they are written on. I'm considering asking that particular MP to conduct a poll among his farmer constituents. I'd like to know how many of them would agree that their wheat should not be sold to Russia or China.

Canadian Manufacturers' Association, Toronto, 8 June 1971

I, personally, am not of the philosophy that because you extend bonds of friendship or of goodwill towards another country you are automatically taking it away from somebody else. This is not my vision of relations between human beings in society and it's not my view of the world.

Town Hall Meeting, London, Ont., 11 November 1971

Defence arrangements

We are discussing here one aspect of a problem which involves the fate of all mankind. I know it is necessary that we, as the government of Canada, must speak about the protection of Canadians, about the protection of our cities, and about the protection we believe our nation deserves. I know, too, that as the government, we must also ensure that the international laws which apply to our air space are respected.

Nevertheless, when I answered questions in the House on this subject the other day I said very frankly that in a real sense these were secondary concerns of ours, and I will explain why this is so. We believe that this whole matter is not one in which only Canadians are involved. I echo what the leader of the New Democratic Party said when I say that we believe that this whole matter is one which involves the fate of humanity. It is for this reason that we on this side of the House take the position that before sitting down to bargain with the United States on where the [ABM] system should be located, on whether they have considered where the fall-out would occur, whether or not it would be on Canadian cities, we want to remain free to say that we condemn this system entirely. We want to be free to disapprove of it, which we would not be if we said to them: 'Please set it down here or there and please make sure that you do not destroy us in the process of protecting yourselves'.

At a Remembrance Day ceremony, London, Ont., 1971

This is the reason that I, and the government, take this stand. When I do speak to the President I will not be in the position of asking for a little more protection for Canadians but rather will be able to put questions to him about whether his decision constitutes an escalation and an increase of the danger of nuclear warfare or whether it is merely an operation which adds to the stability of the deterrent system.

Some years ago Canadians did not have such a difficult decision to make. Other countries in history have lived for years in the fear of destruction, although perhaps not nuclear destruction. Wars in other lands very often constituted an imminent danger of destruction to many nations. For us in Canada, however, it is the first time that we have been faced with such a problem. It is only four and a half decades ago that Senator Dandurand was able to say to the League of Nations that we in Canada 'live in a fireproof house, far from inflammatory materials'.

This is no longer the case. Our house is not fireproof and, as we know, inflammatory materials are no longer very far from it. Science has made us all neighbours in this world. The progress of science and technology is such that one nation cannot hope to save itself alone. Talented writers have used various expressions to express this result. Mr McLuhan speaks about the 'global village', and he is right: we are truly living in a global village. Barbara Ward talks about a 'Spaceship Earth'. I suggest these expressions convey, in a true sense, the feeling of solidarity that we as Canadians have with all nations on this earth.

We might, of course, protest that they should not be using our air space or that they should not contemplate exploding anti-ballistic missiles over Canadian soil. However, I repeat, as I said the other day in the House, that this would be a fairly academic consideration, Mr Speaker, because should the system begin to fire it will mean our efforts to preserve the peace and the safety of the world have failed, and I think the question of national air space would be secondary.

House of Commons, 19 March 1969

Canada's NATO relationship is not, primarily, a military decision. It is a political decision. As such the Canadian government is acting in a responsible fashion when it observes that the European members of NATO now have a combined population of 300 millions, and a combined gross national product of 500 billion United States dollars. The remarkable post-World War II recovery of the states of Western Europe has increased considerably their capability of defending their own region. This increased capability in turn reduces the present need for a sustained Canadian military contribution.

I might emphasize as well that, apart from the United States, Canada is at present the only member of NATO which is carrying out an extensive NATO military role on two continents. In summary, we feel that Europe, twenty years after NATO, can defend itself better and we hope that NATO's European member countries, with the support of the United States and Canada, can reach some agreement with the Warsaw Pact countries to de-escalate the present tension. For our part we are not now advocating a reduction of NATO's total military strength, although we hope that this may become possible, but a readjustment of commitments among NATO members.

It follows, and our defence review has made it clear, that a Canadian military presence in Europe is not important so much on the grounds that we fulfil a military role as we do a political role. We contribute in some measure to the 'resolve' of the organization, to the will of the Alliance to respond to any aggression. This being the case, the Canadian military function in NATO may be seen to be a manifestation of our political policy.

This is consistent with one of the important roles of NATO, which is political – the accommodation with the Warsaw Pact countries of the outstanding differences between the two alliances and agreement on arms control and arms limitation.

It is this search for détente which is one of the compelling reasons for remaining a member of NATO. Quite apart from any military role, there is, we believe, an important political role for NATO and for Canada within NATO in this attempt to remove or reduce the underlying political causes of potential conflict through steps toward political reconciliation and settlement.

The efforts expended in search of a secure Canada and a peaceful world in the last 25 years are in some ways inappropriate for the next 25 years ... Following the same careful type of study and with the same resolve that launched Canada in 1945 into a then new and effective role in the world, we believe Canada is now on the threshold of another new role. This does not mean, however, that our present posture or our present attitude must necessarily be totally changed.

It is obvious from the foregoing that the government has rejected, for example, any suggestion that Canada assume a non-aligned or neutral role in the world. To do so would have meant the withdrawal by Canada from its present alliances and the termination of all co-operative military arrangements with other countries. That would be wrong; it is necessary and wise to continue to participate in an appropriate way in collective security arrangements with other states in the interests of Canada's national security and in defence of the values we share with our friends.

The precise military role which we shall endeavour to assume in these collective arrangements will be a matter for discussion and consultation with our allies and will depend in part on the role assigned to Canadian forces in the defence of North America in co-operation with the United States. They will be consistent as well with our belief that, as a responsible member of the international community, we must continue to make forces available for peace-keeping roles.

The world, Mr Speaker, is embarked upon a revolutionary period which dwarfs by comparison the changes of the past centuries. Our era combines a technological revolution with a revolution of rising expectations of billions of people who for the first time in history are projecting themselves to the forefront of our consciences as they seek their proper place in the international community. This is the excitement, this is the challenge, recognized by so many of our youth.

We as Canadians would not be fulfilling our potential for good if we remained aloof from these events. This government intends to reorganize our resources and our energies to play a role in the world as it is, not to dream of things as they were. Those in this House and elsewhere who say that our defence policy represents a turn toward isolationism are proclaiming only that, in their fixation on old wars and on old problems, they are isolated – isolated from the world of now and the world of the future.

Canada has the opportunity to play a role in the world of today, Mr Speaker, a role which, hopefully, will act as an incentive to other like-minded states, a role which will emphasize the need to devote energies to the reduction of tension and the reversal of the arms race – a role which will acknowledge that humanity is increasingly subject to perils from sources in addition to an east-west conflict centred in Europe, and which will permit us to make the intellectual and resource investments necessary to do our part to meet those perils. This is why we are insisting that our defence policy be directed by our foreign policy, and not vice versa. This is why we are placing emphasis on imaginative concepts of assistance to developing countries. This is why we are insisting that our defence policy be rational and not a rationalization.

The government, Mr Speaker, recognizes that the challenge of future world social and political events will not be met by a stagnant cautious attitude. We must anticipate, not react; we must think, not conform; we must have courage to discard conventional wisdom in our quest for a secure and peaceful world. If this requires change, so be it.
House of Commons, 23 April 1969

The threat to the human race is so real that we must not permit false reasoning to hinder us in our endeavours. If the application of out-of-date military strategies to alliances with old and trusted friends might lead not to the desired deterrent effect but instead to provocation and to obstacles to détente, then these strategies must be re-examined. In these instances it is the strategy, not the alliance, that worries Canada, and we will not hesitate to suggest correctives with the same vigour that we contributed to the establishment of the alliance.
House of Commons, 24 October 1969

The United States

Q   To some extent your change of administration with the elections, and your entering the office of Prime Minister is parallel to what is happening in the United States; only a period of perhaps eight months will separate this assumption of power by yourself and by Mr Nixon. Do you intend to meet with him with a view of re-examining and possibly readjusting relations between Canada and the United States?

A   Well, I can only answer a general intention there. I have no specific intention to meet with him. There has been no exchange of any kind of information along those lines. But I would hope that Mr Nixon and I would be able to discuss these questions and many others. I think the foremost thing I have to discuss when I meet responsible leaders of friendly countries is not so much specifics of this, that or the next thing, and I believe a lot of this can be left to our diplomatic personnel and to our civil servants in the area of Trade and Commerce and so on. I would like to try and understand what the major premises of Mr Nixon's thinking are, and I would like to acquaint him with mine. I would like to know what he is thinking about the future – not just thinking because he has talked a great deal – but what his basic postulates or premises are about the future of this North American continent for the next twenty years. What are the dangers; what are the hopes; in what direction is the population moving; what will we do with urban growth; what will we do with problems of economic interdependence; what will we do with the multi-national corporation; what will we do in the United Nations? But not in specifics. How does he see the world? Does he think about China as I do, that it's probably more in their interest to be in the long run friendly with the United States than friendly with Russia? What does he think about the problem of the black people in the United States and how does he think this is going to be solved in the next several years? Is he very concerned with problems of poverty in the third world? What priorities does he put on international aid and development as against shooting for the moon? But these are things that I find interesting discussing with anyone, therefore I would find it even more interesting discussing them with the President of the United States.

Q May I ask some specific questions: first, are you worried about the influx of American capital investment in the sense that this investment might result in an American economic domination of this country? And if so, do you plan any restrictions on American capital investment in Canada?

A Well, I am not worried in the sense that I don't worry over something which is somewhat inevitable, and I think the problem of economic domination is somewhat inevitable, not only of the United States over Canada but perhaps over countries of Europe as well, and the problems of the economic domination of Japan over some countries in the Far East, and the problem of economic domination of the Soviet Union over some of the smaller countries around it and so on. These are facts of life, and they don't worry me. I would want to make sure that this economic presence does not result as I say in a real weakening of our national identity. I use that general expression too. The way in which I do that is to try and balance the benefits against the disadvantages. It is obvious if we keep out capital and keep out technology, we won't be able to develop our resources and we would have to cut our standard of consumption in order to generate the savings to invest ourselves, and so on. Once again, I think even more important than the capital which comes in from the United States is the technology that comes in with it, and we can't have one without the other and we are willing to take both, but on certain conditions. I realize that – you know, I am stating such platitudes ...

Q On the contrary, it is very interesting.

A You realize that each country wants to keep its identity – or its sovereignty, to speak in legal terms. It has to constantly make assessments, and when we make assessments it is to try and select those areas which are important for our independence, for our identity, and some examples are quite obvious – our banking and our financial institutions, and the communications media where we've adopted in the area of radio broadcasting the same kind of laws that you have in the United States, which ensure that control of the media will not belong to foreigners. But we have limited resources, both intellectual and manpower and financial. Therefore the great problem for a government of our size is to know where we will invest those resources most – resources for protecting our identity.

Q How do you feel Canada's relations with the United States should evolve?

A Well, you don't want a long monologue. Would you like me to try and answer in terms of our economic relations? I have a very great respect for the United States and its institutions. I think it is an extraordinarily powerful society. It's vital. It's a tough society, in the good sense of the word. It has lived through difficult problems and I'm sure it has the wherewithal to answer difficult questions. As a student of the law I would say that I have in particular a very great respect for the legal thought that you have developed there – I'm not talking of public law-making, but of the institutions which grew out around your political institutions, the Supreme Court, the federal system of government and so on.

So, I think we are very fortunate to have as a neighbour this very great country. It has obvious economic benefits, it has obvious technological benefits, it has obvious cultural benefits. Even in terms, I suppose, of peace it has obvious benefits; we are in a sense sheltered by the United States' umbrella. But all these assets obviously are counterbalanced by the fact that it is such a large and strong power that in the kind of good neighbour relationship that has existed for a long while, the little guy always feels the rough edges more sensitively than the big guy does, and we have to be careful lest the economic benefits we draw from our relations with the United States lead to a form of economic domination which would lead to atrophy of our political independence. We have to make the same assessment in the area of international relations, that what we gain by having such a strong big brother – I say that in a non-Orwellian sense – we lose by the fact that we cannot be a hundred per cent independent. Of course no country can, not even the United States, but perhaps the measure of our independence is considerably reduced.

In the cultural field it is obvious too. I believe that the benefit that I have underlined, underscored, in the legal field can be extended to many other fields: the intellectual presence of the great universities, the cultural dynamism of a city like New York.

Interview with Jay Walz, New York Times, *22 November 1968*

Canada is, as you know, now reaching the conclusion of the first methodical and total review of our foreign policy and our defence policy since the end of World War II. We have gone back to first principles in doing so, and we are questioning the continuing validity of many assumptions.

Some policies will, without question, be found wanting for the conditions of today and be changed. Others will be retained. I want to emphasize that this review is not an excuse to prove our independence; that independence needs no proving. Nor is it an exercise intended to illustrate to the United States our potential for irritation. We have no desire, and no surplus energy, for that kind of activity.

We are building a new society in Canada. It should not be surprising that the external manifestations of this society may be somewhat different than has been the case in the past. But just as one of the invariable principles of that domestic society is the primacy of the individual, so is one of the invariables of our foreign policy genuine friendship with the United States.

The usual way of stating this fact is to refer in somewhat grandiloquent terms to our 4,000-mile unguarded border, to our lengthy history of amity and harmony, and to the many projects in which we are jointly engaged. It could also be illustrated by proving how interdependent our two nations are in economic, in resource, in geographic, and in environmental terms.

I prefer, however, to express all this more on the level of hockey and Charlie Brown. One of our better-known humourists, Stephen Leacock, put things in their proper perspective. Writing as an English-speaking person in a bilingual society, he said: 'In Canada we have enough to do keeping up with two spoken languages without trying to invent slang, so we just go right ahead and use English for literature, Scotch for sermons, and American for conversation'.

Mr Chairman, so long as we continue to behave like this, I think the warmth with which Canadians and Americans regard each other will protect us all from any sins our governments might in error commit.

As an example to others we hope that we are able on occasion to serve a beneficial purpose. Our close relationship with the United States is an important illustration of what I mean. The fact that Canada has lived and flourished for more than a century as the closest neighbour to what is now the greatest economic and military power in the history of the world is evidence to all countries of the basic decency of United States foreign policy.

And I add in all seriousness that every occasion on which our policies differ from yours in an important fashion, that difference – if of course it is founded on good faith and sound evidence, as we hope is always the case – contributes to your international reputation as a good citizen as much as it does to ours.

When Canada continues to trade in non-strategic goods with Cuba, or proposes the recognition of the Peoples' Republic of China, or – as sometimes happens – finds itself supporting a point of view different from yours in the United States, the world is given evidence of your basic qualities of understanding and tolerance.

Let me say that it should not be surprising if our policies in many instances either reflect or take into account the proximity of the United States. Living next to you is in some ways like sleeping with an elephant: No matter how friendly and even-tempered is the beast, one is affected by every twitch and grunt.

There must be few countries in the world where individuals on either side of a border feel so much at home on the other. I hasten to add, however, that at times in our history we have paused to wonder whether your friendly invitations 'to come and stay awhile' have not been aimed at Canada as a political unit rather than at Canadians as individuals.

Many of you will recall, I am sure, that your Articles of Confederation, as ratified in 1781, contained a clause which was an open invitation, and an exclusive one to Canada. And I read Article IV: 'Canada acceding to this confederation, and joining in the measures of the United States, shall be admitted into, and entitled to all the advantages of this union; but no other colony shall be admitted into the same unless such admission be agreed to by nine states'. So we have always had a favoured position. In any event, we did not join, and history has recorded our differences.

Two hundred years later, the results of our separate and distinct political existence are evident for all the world to see: professional hockey is a major spectator sport from New York to Los Angeles, and 'Peanuts' is one of the most popular comic strips from Halifax to Vancouver.

But Americans should never underestimate the constant pressure on Canada which the mere presence of the United States has produced. We are a different people from you. We are a different people partly because of you.

Our two countries have pushed against one another from time to time, perhaps more courteously in recent years than previously, when your invitation and your republicanism appeared more intimidating to us.

Canadians still smart when they recall President Theodore Roosevelt's tough instructions to Oliver Wendell Holmes Jr, on the occasion of the Alaska-Yukon boundary arbitration. But how many of your historians have ever noted what Canada's first Prime Minister, Sir John A. Macdonald, was at one time contemplating as your fate?

In 1867 that gentleman wrote to a correspondent in Calcutta: 'War will come some day between England and the United States, and India can do us yeoman's service by sending an army of Sikhs, Gheorkas and Beluchees across the Pacific to San Francisco, and holding that beautiful and immoral city with the surrounding California as security for Montreal and Canada'.

You see, Mr Chairman, that although Canadians may not always be able to follow through, we should never be sold short on imaginative proposals.

National Press Club, Washington, DC, 25 March 1969

Mr Speaker, I have the pleasure of drawing Your Honour's attention and the attention of all honourable members to the presence in your gallery of several distinguished visitors. I refer to the three astronauts who made up the crew of Apollo 11, Messrs Neil Armstrong, Mike Collins and Edwin Aldrin and their wives.

The venture of these three brave men into the unknown stirred the imagination and the pride of all Canadians. This country is not so old or so well explored, that either the experience of the frontier or the taste of adventure is forgotten. We are close in time and in space to wilderness. In our blood – or perhaps just in our secret desires – is found the spirit of such as Hudson and Cartier, Palliser and Stefansson. The exploits of our visitors today proved that the age of exploration is not over and we are glad. They proved too that there is new meaning in the heavens, and we are better for it. Mr Speaker, we are delighted to have with us these courageous men and their equally brave wives.

House of Commons, 2 December 1969

Q   I wanted to ask you many, many questions about foreign affairs but there simply will not be time, so I will ask the one which interests me most and that is about this massive neighbour of yours, the United States. You once said: 'Living next to the United States is in some ways like sleeping with an elephant, no matter how friendly or even-tempered is the beast, one is affected by every twitch and grunt.' Can I ask you how real is the danger that the elephant is going to roll over and crush you economically, or culturally or socially, that somehow you are likely to lose your independence by being a neighbour of this vast ...

A   Well, it's a constant danger. I think in some ways New Zealanders feel that Australia is an elephant which, fortunately, would get wet if it rolled over on you. But in our case, there's just an imaginary line which is called the border. There's this constant inflow of what you call American culture, American economic domination, American values and so on. And much of Canadian history and Canadian politics has been preoccupied with preserving our identity. Now, obviously when you're contending with an elephant you can't hope to be stronger and better and bigger than the elephant. What you can do is select those areas in which perhaps you can perform better. You know, man is smaller than an elephant but perhaps he has certain talents which the elephant doesn't have.

Q He would have a better brain.

A He might have a better brain; he might be able to work with tools better and so on. I don't think the comparison is too good but it was used in another sense ... But the essence is that we are forced to husband our energies and select those areas where we can be better than the Americans and we must do this not only with our cultural values but with out economic institutions, and this is the whole process of our setting our priorities. Some people, for instance, wanted to buy back Canada – let's get rid of the Americans, buy up all the subsidiaries. We say we just don't have the dough to do it. Let us choose to invest our capital in those areas which are very important for the society of tomorrow. Let's try and be better than the Americans in something or at least as good as them. Let's not try and produce better automobiles because, you know, the automobile has been thought of a long while ago. But let us try to have the best communications satellite in the world, and let us have the best nuclear energy, nuclear motors for producing electricity and so on. And I think these are examples of areas where we are amongst the best in the world. Therefore, we must husband our energies, not only the monetary ones, the financial ones, but the intellectual ones too – and, if we can, be as good or better than the Americans, for instance in the area of producing films. The National Film Board is as good as any film producer in the United States within a specific area of documentaries and so on. Therefore let us channel energies into this, rather than try and be as good as the Americans in all things.

Interview, TV program 'Gallery', New Zealand Broadcasting Commission, Wellington, NZ, 14 May 1970

One of the purposes of my visit [to Washington] was to seek reassurance from the President, and it can come only from him, that it is neither the intention nor the desire of the United States that the economy of Canada become so dependent upon the United States in terms of a deficit trading pattern that Canadians will inevitably lose independence of economic decision. I stated to the President as candidly as I was able the concern which had been expressed in Canada, and indeed by some honourable members, with respect to the character of the US-Canadian relationship. That concern was precipitated, of course, by the introduction on August 15 of the new United States economic policies, but it has been reflected increasingly in recent years by the continuing flow into Canada of American investment with its attendant advantages and disadvantages.

I cannot emphasize too strongly, Mr Speaker, the warmth and the understanding with which President Nixon responded to my questions, and the candid attitude which he revealed. He assured me that it was in the interests of the United States to have a Canadian neighbour not only independent both politically and economically, but also one which was confident that the decision and policies in each of these sectors would be taken by Canadians in their own interests, in defence of their own values and in pursuit of their own goals.

The century-old desire of Canadians to benefit from our North American neighbourhood and to profit from our relations with the United States, while at the same time remaining Canadian to the degree and extent that we choose, was put to the President by me and accepted by him without hesitation or qualification. We are a distinct country, we are a distinct people and our remaining as such is, I was assured, in the interests of the United States and is a fundamental tenet of the foreign policies of that country as expressed by the Nixon administration.

I should add that the President was sensitive to the suggestion that his August 15th policies could be interpreted as evidence that the United States was unable to accept a Canada with a strong trading and current account position vis-à-vis the United States. The interpretation he could understand, but he stated to me forcefully that it was incorrect. I have not the slightest doubt, having spoken to him, that his interpretation is the correct one and will be borne out by events.

House of Commons, 7 December 1971

The
Commonwealth

It is necessary to grasp the basic fact that this is a civil war [in Nigeria] and that the solution of the conflict is for the disputants themselves to find. Outsiders can offer good offices but they cannot enforce a solution except against the will of the parties. In this instance good offices are and have been readily available – from the Secretary-General of the Commonwealth and from the Organization of African Unity – and I hope they will continue to be used. The fact is that there have been talks periodically between the Nigerian authorities and the rebels throughout the entire period of hostilities, with one series lasting several weeks. This shows that it is not enough to bring the parties together to talk or indeed to proclaim the need for a cease-fire. They must be prepared to make the concessions required to reach a peaceful settlement; it is this spirit of conciliation that cannot be imposed from outside.

Canada intends to remain friendly with all the peoples of Nigeria long after this dispute is settled, and to be in a position where we can play a useful role in assisting the African states to meet their problems. Our policies to this date have been designed to ensure that possibility. All information that reaches us from both parts of Nigeria indicates that we are successful to date.

The torment of the Nigerian peoples must be concluded as soon as possible. At the same time, the future welfare of the Nigerian peoples must be protected and assured. We must not permit our anxiety to achieve the first objective to so foul our reputation and hinder our effectiveness that we will not be given by the parties the opportunity to assist in the long-term recovery of Nigeria.

House of Commons, 26 November 1968

To intervene when not asked ... would not be an act of courage, it would be an act of stupidity. There are some thirty countries in Africa south of the Sahara which have achieved independence since 1957. Every one of these emerged into nationhood following a lengthy and anguished colonial history. No single act would be regarded with more hostility by any of them than the unilateral intervention of a non-African state into their affairs. This the member states of the Organization of African Unity have made crystal clear.

It would be wrong, therefore, Mr Speaker, for the Canadian government to assist the Nigerian government militarily, but it would be equally wrong for the Canadian government to assist the rebel régime politically. Each is an act of intervention. Each would be a presumptuous step, an arrogant step for a country so distant as Canada.

House of Commons, 27 November 1968

This is perhaps the greatest strength of the Commonwealth, this opportunity on a regular basis for men of goodwill to sit down together and discuss one with another the problems which affect them and the 850 million peoples whom they represent. All the other advantages of the Commonwealth relationship – the exchanges of people, the trading patterns, the economic assistance and co-operation schemes, the informality of diplomatic representation – these all assume their tone from the free and frank dialogue which takes place at the Prime Ministerial meetings.

The case of Rhodesia's African neighbours and those who supported them was argued with great vigour and skill; nothing material was omitted in order to avoid hurting the feelings of others; there was no hypocritical attempt to paper over glaring differences and pretend they did not exist. The Rhodesian debate was honest and it was tough – yet at its conclusion something of considerable significance occurred. After looking at the problem in its exact dimensions, after closing in on its many difficulties, men holding opposite views admitted that the true nature of the difficulties was now better understood than before and noted in some instances that their rigid attitudes were capable of some modifications after listening to the comments of others. Of most importance, however, honourable men agreed honourably to disagree.

There is little headline material in the kind of decision; neither is there much domestic political advantage for individual leaders. But to a world burdened almost beyond endurance by incredibly complex problems of immense moment, an agreement to disagree and to search patiently for solutions and areas of agreement is of immeasurable value. Delegates can walk out of meetings in anger. But they cannot remove with them the underlying cause of their annoyance. Organizations can be broken apart by impatient members, but the act of disintegration contributes nothing to the easing of the original tensions.

As the Commonwealth grows in number of members it increases in diversity. The common ingredients, which were once the adhesive of membership, are now outnumbered by the unique institutions and practices of so many of the members. Nor, wisely in my view, have any steps been taken to create some artificial adhesive or binder. There is no charter, no constitution, no headquarters building, no flag, no continuing executive framework. Apart from the secretariat, which is a fraction of the size one might expect for an organization which encompasses a quarter of the peoples on this earth, there is nothing about the Commonwealth that one can grasp or point to as evidence of a structure. Even the use of the word 'organization' creates an impression of a framework which is misleading. The Commonwealth is an organism, not an institution – and this fact gives promise not only of continued growth and vitality, but of flexibility as well.

If this peculiar characteristic of the Commonwealth offers difficulty – as it seems to do – to historians, or journalists, or persons from non-Commonwealth countries it is perhaps unfortunate. But surely this unique source of strength should not

be surrendered in the name of conformity to accepted institutional practices. The Commonwealth is not a miniature United Nations Organization; the Conference is not a decision-making body. To attempt to convert it would simply underscore differences of opinion; it would force countries to take sides and to vote against one another. There exist international organizations where this has to be done and where it is done; the Commonwealth is not and should not become a replica of them.

The Commonwealth provides an opportunity for men of goodwill to discuss with one another – both in plenary session and in the many bilateral meetings – their problems and their hopes for the future; to learn from the wisdom and experience of others. The Commonwealth Conference is a forum for men who are as different as God has made them. It is a meeting place where men are able to demonstrate the advantages of dissimilarity, the richness of diversity, the excitement of variety. Is this not what life is all about, to learn, to share, to benefit, and to come to understand?

I think it is. I think Canadians agree with me, for in our own country we exhibit a multiplicity of character, a diversity of climate, of topography, of resources, of customs, of traditions, of peoples, which is a segment of the wide world beyond. We accept almost instinctively the view that of the many challenges offered by the twentieth century, none is greater than the aspiration of men to live in societies where tolerance and equality are realities. The Commonwealth is a means towards such a goal. To suggest, as some do, that the Commonwealth must be more than a forum for discussion or a clearing house for economic assistance from the few rich nations to the many poor ones, is to miss the vital point of the exercise. Is Canada any less strong, and less united because Canadians and their leaders engage in constant dialogue, because the wealthier provinces accept the principle of tax equalization? I think not.

So too in the broader international community of the Commonwealth. Human inequality is a political fact of great potency. The most effective means of reducing the explosive po-

At the Commonwealth Conference, Singapore, January 1971

tential of discrimination is to meet other persons as political equals and to assist them towards economic equality. That is what the Commonwealth does. I believe these are useful exercises. For these reasons, Mr Speaker, I assured the London Conference that Canada firmly supported the Commonwealth principle.

House of Commons, 20 January 1969

Of all our links, however, perhaps that of the Commonwealth is the most satisfying. The Commonwealth organization, if it may be called that, really has no basic justification for existing. Yet that is the secret of its strength. The Commonwealth exists because of the mutual desire of the peoples of almost thirty independent countries to have their leaders meet periodically as friends. Those meetings have been described as the oldest established, permanent floating summit in the world. The Commonwealth offers us a window on the world. There is no such thing as the 'role' of the Commonwealth. As time passes, however, it may well prove to be the most important of all international bodies simply because it has no role, and because it emphasizes nothing but the importance of the human relationship.

State Dinner, Kuala Lumpur, Malaysia, May 1970

This, Mr Chairman, as several of our colleagues have already stated, is a decade of change; it is rapidly acquiring as well the reputation of a decade of violence. We cannot prevent change. Are we able to contain violence? We must all hope that we can. In order to do so, however, we dare not pursue only the short-term issues however urgent and serious they may be. Nor dare we be content to administer only to the symptoms of the serious diseases that afflict the world. Governments will retain their credibility as instruments of orderly change only if we face up to the underlying problems.

Perhaps for lack of understanding – perhaps because a familiar problem, no matter how bitter, appears preferable to an unknown one – we tend in international gatherings to concentrate on the near future. As political leaders, we face competing and often contradictory demands upon the time and upon the physical resources of our governments. In setting priorities the temptation, indeed the political imperative, favours often the immediate problem at the expense of the long-range, the urgent instead of the important. Both, however, require balancing ...

As we consider the shape of our association in the seventies, we might, I suggest, reflect on whether we want the Commonwealth to become a miniature United Nations, where we spend our time making set-piece speeches rather than talking to each other. The former purpose, it seems to me, is already more than adequately served by existing international forums. As I see it, this unique meeting might more profitably be used for dialogue with one another, with the aim of learning from one another's experience, of broadening our understanding of the forces at work in the world, and of co-operating and seeking ways of dealing with problems which are already looming over the horizon. We would all benefit, I am sure, through taking counsel together, seeking to identify the factors causing change in the world, and helping one another in seeking solutions to some of the issues which we all face. As I see it, there would be mutual advantage in concentrating less on immediate problems which, while important, are for the most part dealt with in other forums, and more on the longer term, focusing at a stage where there is some prospect of influencing the forces at work, and well before the problems assumed the proportions of crises which threaten to overwhelm us. Some of these problems are of course economic disparities, racial discrimination, changing patterns of trade, environmental pollution, and population, to mention only a few of the more obvious. We cannot deal with any of those problems of such momentous proportions by mere reference to them in a general speech, or by short-term arguments relating to an immediate problem, whatever its urgency.

Commonwealth Prime Ministers' Conference, Singapore, January 1971

Canada, measured in terms of political nationhood, is many years older than the State of Pakistan; yet measured in terms of human experience is much, much younger. Recorded history of man's activity in my country measures back only four centuries, and evidence of human experience before that is only fragmentary. In Pakistan, and particularly here in the Indus Valley, men have been present and civilizations have flourished for thousands of years. Tomorrow, at Taxila, I shall see the portrayal of much of this drama in one of the world's most interesting museums.

At Taxila, conqueror replaced conqueror and each laid waste to all his predecessor's achievements. This brutal technique of war was by no means practised only in Asia. In all parts of the world, and in some parts still, there has been repeated again and again the barbaric practice of not only defeating an enemy or the occupier of some sought-after territory, but as well of destroying all evidence of his presence. Measured in terms of human misery this is a horrible practice; as an affront to mankind's previous achievements, the loss is immeasurable.

Islamabad, Pakistan, 7 January 1971

I have not yet been in India three full days on this visit, yet the ambience of this country is so insistent, the sensations so pervasive, that in this short time I have been impressed again with the wisdom, the perception and the devotion which are the heritage of this ageless land. Three days are so many grains of sand in the hour-glass of a lifetime, but they have renewed for me many of my memories of India – and given me glimpses of much that I had not seen before. Three days have left me, as on my previous visits, with an intense desire to return, to see, and to learn what this society and those that have preceded it offer to the world beyond your shores.

One need not journey to Arunachala to celebrate the triumph of light over darkness; that triumph is evident in many parts of India, and recorded in a variety of ways. The day before yesterday at Agra, Brindaban and Mathura, and again at Larnath, I saw testimony of man's devotion to ideals so pure in concept that their appeal is eternal. At Varanasi – and I expect this afternoon at Nehru University – there is evidence of a different sort: evidence of a determination to employ technology and science for the betterment of the peoples of this great country.

The people of both our countries could benefit from an honest acceptance of the reality of the world as it is today, not as it was in yesteryear.

Amrita Pritam has written of the past; two of her lovely lines of poetry read:

> Thy eyes are heavy with dreams,
> Dreams of days gone by ...

Amrita would not ignore the past, any more than we should. But neither would she avoid the future. Nor should we. Both India and Canada must seek and benefit from the windows of the world which are available to us. One of those windows is the Commonwealth. That unique association, possessing no structure and little of an institutional nature, permits us to meet, to visit one another, and to exchange views on an entirely informal and frank basis. The Commonwealth is a product of man's desire to live in peace with his fellow inhabitants of this planet, and of his genius for pragmatic arrangement. I regard it as valuable and worth preserving.
Prime Minister Gandhi's luncheon, New Delhi, India
12 January 1971

The meeting was, as the House is aware, the first regular Commonwealth Conference to take place outside of London, and the first at the head-of-government level to be sited in Asia. I think that an Asian location was most fortunate, partly because it was in Asia that momentum was first initiated for the Commonwealth to be transformed from its older, more confining structure into the widely representative association which it is today, and partly because an Asian situs permitted conference delegates to live and work in a newly independent community in which racial harmony is a necessary fact of life. The world, as we know but so often tend to forget in the immediacy of our own domestic problems, is populated to an overwhelming degree by persons who are desperately poor and whose colonial experience in many instances leads them to question the values and the sincerity of the developed countries. All too often as well, 'rich' and 'white' are regarded by them as synonymous. We forget these facts at our peril.

In Singapore it quickly became apparent that the future of

the world will not necessarily be determined in accordance with European conceptions. The Commonwealth, viewed from Singapore, presented challenges to the ingenuity and goodwill of its members to find ways of communicating across differences measured in many instances by thousands of miles and by centuries of experience, yet without insisting upon adherence to preconceived notions or attitudes. In the result, the value of the Singapore conference might best be described in terms of the comprehension gained by delegates, and not by the persuasion which anyone attempted to exercise.

It is my view now, Mr Speaker, as it was prior to Singapore, that Canada could get along without the Commonwealth but it remains my strong view that we could not get along nearly so well. No problems would be solved by the break-up of the association; not one member would find it easier to advance its own interests in its absence. The Commonwealth benefits all members and harms none. It is my firm expectation that with the help of the important Commonwealth Declaration the association will prove to be a major contributor to the enrichment of human relations. Commonwealth members share a common language. Even more important, they share a common idiom. In the result, there is permitted an informality of encounter and a meeting of minds that surely must be the envy of other countries.

Canada cannot live apart from the world. Events in far-off places do affect us, as we have seen again and again in our history. If we are able to influence those events for the better, through attendance at important international conferences, and through meetings with heads of friendly states, then it is the duty of Canada to attempt to do so. This duty does not flow from some vague international role to be played by Canada. Canada must act according to how it perceives its aims and interests. It is in our interest that there not be a general racial war in Africa, in the near or distant future. If the Commonwealth Conference reduced the chances of such a war, and if the Canadian delegation contributed to the success of that conference, then I submit, Mr Speaker, that the effort was well expended.

House of Commons, 1 February 1971

The Threshold
of Greatness

A land for people

We are fortunate people, we Canadians who live in this land. And our greatest good fortune, that which is becoming increasingly evident to others even if not always to ourselves, is not measured in terms of economic or political or military strength. It is more valuable than the sum of all of these. It is the greatest of our natural resources. It is the tolerance towards one another which forms such a basic part of the character of Canadians.

Tolerance and moderation are found in this country perhaps in larger measure than anywhere else; against them we can judge our stature as a country and as a people. Our institutions of government and our judiciary have long encouraged a climate of non-interference of Canadians towards Canadians. We are all the richer for it. We here take for granted what many others seek and envy: relationships that by and large accept without question differences in colour or origin or language, and a common resolution to eliminate whatever intolerance does exist.

This, surely, is the strength of Canada. This is the heritage of Canadians. To enjoy the opportunity to live in dignity as individuals, to share freedom of thought and expression and movement, to seek happiness each in our own way. This spirit we all share, from this spirit we all benefit.
Message to the Nation, 1 July 1969

At Sept-Iles, September 1970

Is there some mysterious force in our character which drives us relentlessly in this introspective quest for our identity? Or is it just that in our assemblage along the United States border we have turned away from that great mass of Canada lying to the north, and in so doing set up a tension between our minds and our hearts? If this be the case, how unnecessary is our uncertainty. For if there is a distinctive Canadian characteristic, surely it is an awareness of space – a dynamism of spirit prompted by our sense of the frontier.

These are not recent phenomena; space has always been part of our lives. For many years we looked to our western frontier for excitement and for opportunity. Now we look to another frontier – to the north – for some sense of our purpose both as individuals and as a country. The frontiers of Canada have been as rugged and as challenging as those anywhere in the world, but in certain important respects they reflect distinctively Canadian characteristics. Violence was not commonplace in our west, for example, and it is not part of our north. In Canada the law preceded the cattleman and the prospector. In the result we have been deprived of the raw materials for a 'western' movie industry. But we have been left with something of much greater value. In place of gun-toting sheriffs and vigilante citizens, we have a respect for law and orderly processes; in place of a fanatical right-wing brand of individualism we have a sense of tolerance and a built-in accommodation for varying points of view. These are not the usual legacies of a frontier, and none of us should underestimate the value of their benefits to us.

Not unexpectedly, perhaps, Canadians seldom attempt to explain even to themselves their spiritual attachment to the wilderness. We are occupied in other directions. But one who has done so, and with more perception than most, was my canoeing companion and your colleague, Blair Fraser. Blair wrote that: 'What held such people together was not love for each other; it was love of the land itself, the vast empty land in which for more than three centuries, a certain type of man has found himself uniquely at home'. Blair often said that it was necessary for him, from time to time, to leave the cities and strike out into the quiet in order to understand what Canada was all about and what made life in this country so singularly exciting and satisfying.

At Resolute, one is closer to Lenigrad than to Los Angeles; Alert is closer to Oslo than Edmonton is to New York; and Inuvik is less distant from northern Japan than is Victoria from St John's. From high in the Arctic, Canada and its twenty-two million people crowded along the United States border look somehow different than they do from further south.

From here in the north one can see that Canadian society is distinguishable from that in many other countries; we have never expected that each of us should be melted into replicas of one another; our standard of living is higher than most others.

Here in the Arctic, one needs no explanation of Canada. Here, no one doubts that the circumstances of space and need and trust have combined to create an atmosphere which often brings out the best in men. The wilderness encourages a reluctance to selfishness, a stimulus to self-confidence, and a reticence to find fault with others. Here, there is no inhibition about destiny or purposes, no assumption that good fortune is either preordained or inaccessible. Self-deception gives way quickly in the Arctic; sham proves no match for integrity.

The qualities and values which are so evident in the north are equally present, even if not so visible, elsewhere in Canada. Perhaps the source of those qualities, however, is the north, as Blair Fraser believed when he said that our north was 'too barren ever to be thickly settled, too bleak to be popular', but that 'there is no reason to doubt that it will always be there, and so long as it is there, Canada will not die'.

The professional pessimists among us say that we are all doubts and visions and confusions; that we are a youth suffering from the difficulties of adolescence.

Let them moan; it is the unimaginative and the frustrated who are always the first to despair about the attitudes of the young. Youth is hope and adventure and confidence. And so is Canada. It is youth, not the pessimists who sing in this city every night – plus matinées on Sundays – of 'harmony and understanding, sympathy, and trust abounding'.

This land is vibrant with young men and women challenging the world and accomplishing deeds that their grandparents would not have dreamed possible. In a number of fields young Canadians are doing their own things and doing them brilliantly. There is little doubt why they have neither the time nor the interest to read or heed the laments and gloomy prognostications that some of their long-faced elders put on paper from time to time. Nor would anyone be more mystified than youngsters to learn that others in this country are preaching not excellence, but chauvinism; not competition, but xenophobia.

Canadians are not inhibited or directed by pressures of manifest destiny. Our destiny is what we choose to make it. And if we surprise ourselves from time to time by our own accomplishments, so what? If we find that there is fun in being Canadian, why not?

I have likely given too much credit to the pessimists. It may be that it is not the anxieties of the cautious and the fearful, but rather the weight of January, that causes some Canadians regularly to despair. Perhaps winter stays with us too long and our hang-ups are nothing more than manifestations of wintertime melancholy. If so, then spring is all the more exhilarating when it does arrive. 'I heard the spring wind whisper', wrote Bliss Carman; 'I heard the spring rain murmur'. We all do. Never are our ears more sensitive than at this time of the year.
Annual Meeting, Canadian Press, Toronto, 15 April 1970

Q Why have you been such an outstanding opponent of separatism in Canada?
A Oh, many, many reasons. One of them is that I think the country itself is one of the countries in the world which has the greatest potential for creating a society in which quality of men's lives is foremost in government's minds. We haven't yet reached the stage of industrial production where we are obsessed with material goods, though we are obsessed a great deal, but we are not obsessed only by that. I think Canada has a population of a manageable size. It is still possible to convince the majority of the people of the relevance of government. It is still possible to discuss with them the difficulties of the problems and the intricacies of the solutions. It is a manageable

country yet, and for this I think we could be in the forefront of reform in all the areas, not only economic and social but in the areas of the Criminal Code we were talking about, penitentiary reform, reform of legislation, reform of industrial production, a different distributive mechanism, and so on. There are so many things to do. The country interests me as a Canadian I suppose.

Now, why am I such an opponent of separatism? I guess I just feel that the challenge of the age is to live together with people who don't have all the same values as yourself. I believe in pluralistic societies. I believe that the way of progress is through the free exchange of ideas and confrontation of values. Separatism is really an ethnocentric-based society which says all the French must live together, and all the Scottish, and all the Welsh, and all the Irish, and there should be no intercommunication between them except at the official level of the state. I think that the wealth of a society and the wealth of a country like Canada, and no doubt New Zealand, is that we have immigrants who come from all parts of the world, and we have people who were there before we arrived like the Indians and the Eskimos. And the challenge is to have all these values challenge each other in terms of excellence, and it is this challenge which permits a society to develop on the basis of excellence.

Interview, TV *program 'Gallery', New Zealand Broadcasting Commission, Wellington, NZ, 14 May 1970*

We have seen in recent weeks how deep is the belief in Canada, and how widespread is the understanding of the benefits that accrue to each of us as Canadians.

We have seen the face of despair; we have encountered the effects of violence. We have sworn as one people to drive them both from our land. We have acknowledged with pride and without hesitation that we are Canadians; that this is a land of tolerance, a community of understanding. We accept without hesitation that Canada is a land for people. So must it remain.

The aim of the government throughout has been consistent: to make Canada and life in Canada more attractive; to contri-

bute to the quality of the lives of Canadians of this and future generations. In doing so we have emphasized the value of a society comprised of two major linguistic communities, made richer with the cultural contributions of native Canadians and groups from half a hundred regions of the world, and pursuing a life style which is characterized by goodwill, tolerance and compassion. We should never doubt that we are Canadians – that we are different.
Liberal Policy Conference, Ottawa, 20 November 1970

You are all familiar, I am sure, with the statements made by some observers that Canada is one of the most difficult countries in the world to govern. The reasons that these persons give in support of their argument are several: our vast size; our relatively small and widely dispersed population; the vivid disparities in distribution of natural resources; the presence of two major linguistic communities. It may be true that some – certainly not all – smaller, more homogenous countries have fewer problems. But I'm sure that they are much less exciting places in which to live, with far fewer challenges and many fewer opportunities.
Service Club Council of Saint John, NB, 8 December 1970

Happy New Year, 1971. The Centennial of British Columbia; the 104th year of Confederation; the 178th year since Alexander Mackenzie crossed the continent to reach the Pacific by land; the 299th year since Dollier and Galinée penetrated inland as far as Sault Ste Marie; the 395th year since Martin Frobisher sailed into the Bay on Baffin Island that bears his name; the 436th year since Jacques Cartier ascended the St Lawrence as far as Montreal.

These dates all mark significant events in Canadian history. They remind us that this land of ours has a long and colourful past, one rich with the contributions of daring English and French explorers whose names and feats are familiar to all of us: Champlain, Hudson, La Vérendrye, Henday, Fraser, and scores of others. By no historic measurement can we claim that Canada is a young land; nearly 500 years have passed since John Cabot sighted Newfoundland.

Yet if there is one characteristic that is common to Canadians, it is that we think of Canada as a young country. I hope we always will. To be young is to be full of hope and imagination and vigour. To be young is to be confident; it is also to be questioning and concerned.

These are the characteristics of Canada and Canadians. From coast to coast there are millions of persons of all ages in this country who think and act in youthful terms. Many Canadians are, of course, young. On them we rely for a bold and satisfying future for our land.

Canada can be what our children wish of it if we do not deprive them first of their normal childhood instincts; their active curiosity; their friendly nature; their natural tolerance; their desire to learn and to create. If we permit our children to share with us their vitality, we shall feel within us that Canada can be as exciting and as human a country as we wish it to be. If we look into the eyes of children and see others with their help, we will notice many conditions in Canada that must be changed: poverty, ignorance, discrimination. But we will also identify many other traits that we want to preserve because they contribute to the kind of Canada we desire: basic attitudes of compassion and tolerance and openness.

New Year's Television Address, 1 January 1971

For years my impressions of the prairies were confined to those I gained as a boy from the strong paintings of western Canadian artists and from the journals of the early explorers. Saskatchewan to me was a land of heroic stature – with horizons unbelievably wide, with skies higher than any I had ever seen and with a raw, natural power sufficient to challenge and repel all but the most disciplined and persevering of men. My impressions had a factual base, for the character of the homesteaders who first settled this province and of those who later came to grips with its size and climate was moulded by interminable distances and inhospitable winters. That individual

At Lunenburg, NS, July 1971

character has since become the provincial character. Today we can see the brilliant results of the efforts of those men and women, and the warm spirit of community co-operation which has been continued through the years.

Liberal Party of Saskatchewan, Regina, 13 February 1971

A country does not achieve greatness by itself, however. It requires the application of human resolve. Opportunities must be seized by people. Promises must be redeemed by individuals.

Our national performance can never exceed the sum of our individual performances. There is no alchemy available to governments (or to statisticians) which can make Canada something other than the product of our talents, our efforts, and our accomplishments. If Canadians, individually, are indifferent – 'copping out' is the expression of the Woodstock generation – then so will be Canada. There can be but a single aim for Canada and for Canadians – a standard of excellence.

Canada is not so wealthy in human or in material resources that we are able to cater to mediocrity in any of its manifestations, or to ignore or misuse the talent in our midst. No society is that wealthy; none has ever so acted without suffering as a result. Canada must somehow offer challenging opportunities to all its citizens and must foster within them the desire to perform well.

One need not look far in this or any other Canadian community to find evidence of low standards and poor performance, of misused or wasted skills. We cannot claim with honesty that our present level of achievement is the best we can attain; that our accomplishments in the arts or in science, in business or in government are adequate. They are not. They are not for several reasons, one of the most unfortunate of which is society's refusal to offer to all Canadians an opportunity to participate and to contribute to the extent that they are capable and to the extent that they desire. This refusal reflects a variety of circumstances – sometimes prejudice, sometimes nepotism, sometimes indifference, sometimes economic fallacy. Whatever the circumstance, however, society suffers and Canada is less than it might otherwise be.

Toronto and District Liberal Association, 3 March 1971

Ministers and their colleagues believe that Canadians continue to cherish the value system which has made them among the most fortunate of all the world's peoples. A system which enhances human relationships – tolerance, friendship, love, laughter, privacy; a system which pays heed to the beauty of our country and seeks to preserve the balance of nature; a system which accepts the inevitability of change but which encourages only those changes which respect, rather than exploit, the human spirit; a system, in short, which regards individuals as the ultimate beneficiaries. We believe that the character of Canada – Canada's nationalism if you will – is not marked or identified by a sense of eighteenth-century territorial grandeur or nineteenth- and early twentieth-century economic ferocity. Canada is known to its inhabitants and to others as a human place, a sanctuary of sanity in an increasingly troubled world. We need not search further for our identity. These traits of tolerance and courtesy and respect for our environment and one another provide it. I suggest that a superior form of identity would be difficult to find.

Infrequent incidents of violence do not alter this atmosphere of tolerance. The overwhelming majority of Canadians from coast to coast are not impressed with this evidence of mental bankruptcy; Canadians prefer order to chaos, and creation to destruction. They believe that problems can be solved, and tomorrow's avoided, through political action. They view violence as a threat, not a solution; nor, I should add, is their mood in tune with perpetual poor-mouthing or professional pessimism.

The Liberal government does not worship either productivity or growth. It works for people. We stand with those who believe that life in Canada can be exciting and rewarding and satisfying – and that the likelihood of all Canadians achieving those goals now and in the future is enhanced by a government which acts with imagination and determination to protect both the individual and his environment.
Liberal Party of Vancouver, 1 May 1971

Ukrainians represent one of a large number of social communities in Canada whose original membership migrated from other countries, and who continue to arrive in large numbers from many parts of the world. In Canada they retain their own folklore and customs, and many have maintained a fluency in their original language through several generations. It is the presence in Canada of this combination of ethnic communities which prompts Canadians to refer to their country as a mosaic. Successive Canadian governments have respected the desire of Canadians to foster their original cultures. Many of these cultures have histories far older than Canada itself; all of them enrich the Canadian experience.

Those of your countrymen now in Canada, Mr Chairman, though many thousands of miles away from the Ukraine, find themselves living within a constitutional framework with a formal structure similar to that in the Soviet Union. Each of our countries has chosen a federal system of government which divides jurisdiction between a national government and governments of the constituent parts. A federal system is perhaps the most complex and least easy to operate of all governmental systems. Nevertheless, its very complexity is its strength, for it permits a necessary degree of flexibility. In states as large as are Canada and the Soviet Union, containing as they do peoples of several different regional and ethnic communities, a federal structure permits a balance to be struck between the national requirement and the local, the common good and the particular interest.

Reply to toast, Kiev, USSR, May 1971

Over the years, Canadians, and among them Canadian businessmen, have made this country work not because it was rational or logical or predestined. They have made it work because they were stubborn enough to disregard the continentalists and the realists and the pessimists. They disregarded the gloomsters just as Japanese businessmen disregarded the gloomy forecasts of their immediate future made in 1945.

Why do the commentators of all breeds feel that it is their duty to convert Canada into a nation of introspective contemplators? Neither this country nor this proud association of yours would have gotten off the ground had that attitude prevailed a century ago. It didn't prevail then and I'm confident that it won't prevail now. I remind you of the words of Cyrus A. Birge, the president of the CMA in 1903. Mr Birge said 'We are manufacturers not merely of articles of wood and stone, and iron and cotton and wool. We manufacture enthusiasms; we manufacture a feeling of pride in our country, a spirit of independence'.

Canadian Manufacturers' Association, Toronto, 8 June 1971

One of the unfortunate aspects of life in a country as large and as burgeoning as Canada is how little each of us knows about the day-to-day contribution of others. What we read in our history books – as in our newspapers – tends most often to be of the adventurous or romantic kind of activity, and very seldom of the disciplined drudgery of man's struggle against adversity. It has been left to the poet and to the novelist to chronicle the heroism of ordinary men in ordinary circumstances, whose contribution comes not from some single act of bravery or inspiration but from the steady application of human resolve in despair as well as in joy. This is not material for a dramatic TV special or a cinematic extravaganza, but it is the very stuff of life, and the secret of the strength of the Canadian character.

The names of explorers – Mackenzie and Radisson, Fraser and La Vérendrye – are known to every school child; the romance of the voyageurs and the buffalo-hunters are spelled out in the history books. But how many Canadians know of such extraordinary feats as the migration in 1887 of the first party of Mormon men, women and children north from Utah over the desolate and forbidding wilderness of Idaho and Montana to found the now prosperous farming and ranching communities of southern Alberta? How many of us have been told of the fortitude of Chief Piapot and his Cree Indian people as they struggled through the bitter winter of 1883-84 when temperatures dropped to 40° below zero? And who but those living in a line from Winnipeg to Edmonton are aware today of the hardship endured, and the difficulties overcome, by those persons, many of Ukrainian origin, who settled the west between 1880 and 1914?

It is a different kind of man, and a different kind of

woman, who strikes out into new terrain, not to discover and pass on, but to settle and develop. Every country requires both explorers and settlers – on the frontiers of the land, on the frontiers of science and industry and business – but it is the settlers who are so often the unsung heroes.

It is difficult for Canadians in 1971 to envisage the harshness and the deprivations overcome by that generation which came to Canada from northern and eastern Europe three-quarters of a century ago. They came to escape the economic, social and political deprivations of other societies, but they encountered here climatic and environmental rigours of a dimension they had never expected, and for which they were ill-prepared. They remained – suffering through bitterly cold winters in crude shelters fashioned of mud, opening to cultivation vast tracts of virgin land, benefitting from the entrepreneurial character of the community, and assuming willingly the responsibilities of a free and democratic society. Canada owes much to them, and not just in regional terms. The contribution of those settlers is felt far away from Minnedosa, or Humboldt, or Mundare. Those settlers, through their hardiness, the retention of their cultures and their values, their understanding of the forces of history, but above all through their fortitude, changed all of Canada.

It is the peculiar attractiveness of Canada and Canadians that we do not encourage the illusory and self-destructive luxury of hatred – either in our relations one with another or towards persons and governments beyond our borders. It is Canada's pluralism that has led to this result and that has permitted us as well to exert some modest influence in the world; an influence guided by idealism but moulded by reality.

Many persons have understood the interaction of these two constraints. Few, however, have felt them so deeply as did Taras Shevchenko. His message is your message; it is a message for us all. He wrote:

> As long as hope still dwells within the heart,
> There let it live, and drive it not away.

We have hope in Canada. We have it partly because we are a classless society. We bring our individual talents from our own cultural backgrounds and we contribute them to the betterment of a land in which equality of opportunity remains as important a factor as do the traits of tolerance and understanding.

Ukrainian-Canadian Congress, Winnipeg, 9 October 1971

Each time I return to this province I attempt to imagine the excitement, the confidence of Nova Scotia a century ago, for then the men and women of this province were participating in a golden age. Graceful ships, skilfully built and skilfully sailed, brought both fame and fortune to the province. The busy yards at Lunenburg were so active that for years Nova Scotia led the world in tonnage launched per capita of population, and Yarmouth held the world's record for ownership per capita. Resourceful sea captains founded a profitable trade in the rich stocks of cod off the Grand Banks, the timber of the Atlantic provinces and the more exotic products of the Caribbean. From Labrador to Florida, only a small handful of Atlantic communities could claim to be cities – with all the factors of industry, culture and prominence that city status demands. And high on that list were two friendly rivals of the north, Halifax and Boston.

In the third quarter of the nineteenth century, Nova Scotia looked to the sea for its livelihood, and found rich returns. Young men and women were proud of their province and confident that its future was bright. Now, today, a century later, Nova Scotia is again looking seaward and I sense here in Halifax the same infectious spirit and air of conviction that must have been present here 100 years ago. I felt it all through the day, in the various groups I met – both the students and the Chamber of Commerce and you here tonight. And I am delighted that this is so. The federal government shares with you the same high hopes and the same sense of attainment that are so widespread in the province today. The expectation that one or more of Canada's Atlantic provinces will become self-sufficient economically is of importance not only to this region of Canada, but to the whole country. Canada will be better for it and all Canadians will be proud that we have come closer to our goal of a land without glaring regional economic disparities ...

Thomas Raddall wrote in his well known book about Halifax that a century or so ago there was 'famous young stuff stirring' in this city. I think that history will show that in the 1970s there was also young stuff stirring, and that the current young stuff is also destined to become famous. As they stir, and engage in the excitement of Nova Scotia in its new age of confidence, they are watched with favour by many ghosts of giant stature – and I'm not referring to that ghost from Halifax who rattles his chains from time to time in Ottawa. I'm referring to the friendly ghosts of long ago – Tom Haliburton, James Gordon Bennett, Sam Cunard, Joseph Howe and others. I can't imagine a more stimulating sensation.

This is a great age for Nova Scotia, Mr Chairman. I'm proud as a Canadian to be part of it.

Nova Scotia Liberal Association, Halifax, 29 October 1971

The image of Canada remains as bright today, I hope, as it did decades ago in the mind of the first immigrant to these shores. That image was of a land of immense economic potential, a land free from the rigidities of social classes and political tyranny, a land so big that it could accommodate the differing ideas and life-styles of millions of men and women, a land where the word 'opportunity' possessed genuine meaning, a land where the individual's worth was not something known only to him and to God but was appreciated and cherished by the entire community. In these respects – and I doubt that any others come close to them in importance – Canada remains as attractive today as at any previous time. Canada is a place where men and women of conviction and passion exercise tolerance and moderation in the pursuit of their goals. Participation is denied to none. Canadians still believe in the institutions which they have created for the betterment of their society and for the governance of their activities. These institutions belong to them, are subject to their wishes, and can be modified by them to meet changing conditions ...

We have in Canada a belief that we can devise here a society as free of prejudice and fear, as full of understanding and love, as respectful of individuality and beauty, as receptive to change and innovation, as exists anywhere. We have no desire

to make Canada a state whose reputation rests only on its power; no wish to appear militaristic in the eyes of others. Canadians seek within this land a society in which they and their children can grow and fulfil themselves as human beings.
Canadian-Italian Business and Professional Men's Association of Toronto, 2 December 1971

You could, of course, go it alone. You could be an independent country here in British Columbia. You have got everything going for you – the people, the scenery, the natural resources, the trading openings – and yet you agree to pay taxes to the federal government so that it can use some of this money to help the less fortunate provinces in the Atlantic area. You accept that through equalization grants our governments come to you as they come to Alberta, as they come to Saskatchewan, as they go to Ontario and take money in order to help to develop other parts of Canada. This is because Canadians want to hold on to every part of this country. This is because there is not a Quebec problem and there is not a Maritime problem; and there is not a French problem and an English problem. There is a Canadian problem and a Canadian future; and that is because we have a federal form of government, it is because we have in Ottawa a strong government which can perform these functions of redistributing wealth from the rich to the poor or from the rich provinces to the poor provinces, not by way of charity, not because of the statistics of higher unemployment in the Atlantic area, not because of the amount of dollars which are lost by being unproductive, but because of the human factor, because of the waste in terms of human values when Canadians everywhere will not have the education or do not have the opportunity to fulfil themselves to the utmost. It is the frustration, it is the human incapability of fulfilling oneself to the utmost which is the tragedy. It is not the economic one as much as the others.

There was a very great French writer called Saint-Exupéry who told the story of travelling through central Europe, and sitting opposite a Polish family with a little boy who seemed very intelligent and very bright, but whose family was very poor, and who knew they would never be able to send him to school. To Saint-Exupéry the face of the little boy was exactly that of Mozart when he was a boy. He called his story the 'Assassination of Mozart', for he knew that this little boy would not be able to grow up into a Mozart because of the economics of the social environment in which he was going to be forced to live.

This problem exists within our own country, and can lead to disunity if we do not face problems together, if we are not willing to consider that we are our brother's keeper in all of Canada, if we are not prepared to involve ourselves in the solution of these problems together.

Fort Langley, BC, 17 June 1968

Canada's future

In this country we may well be on the eve of great accomplishment. We have the opportunity of demonstrating how people of the two great linguistic communities, fortified by the presence of millions who have inherited their own rich traditions, can live together, and prosper, and enrich one another in the process. In this country we have the resources, both physical and human, that will permit us, with determination and discipline, to expand and strengthen our economy. We have traditions of freedom and individual initiative which remind us constantly that the deprivation of the rights of one person is a deprivation of the rights of us all.

We also have the opportunity and the responsibility to ensure that these benefits can be shared in increasing measure by the peoples of the world. If we miss that opportunity, or shirk that responsibility, we fail not only those we seek to assist. We fail ourselves as well.

University of Alberta, Edmonton, 13 May 1968

Q   Do you think Canada as a nation can in fact survive given the racial, regional and economic problems it faces, or is Mr [George] Ball in fact correct when he states that Canada is doomed, no matter what it does, to be swallowed up by our neighbours to the south of us?

A   I will not comment on Mr Ball's assertion, but I will say that we are faced with a very difficult challenge, but much easier than that which faces most industrial societies if you look at them. We have a very advanced technological base. We have one of the richest natural resource countries in the world, but we are faced with these centrifugal forces. The far West – Alberta and British Columbia – is rich and it feels that it in a sense can alienate itself from the rest of Canada because Ottawa is such a far-away government. The eastern provinces are in the opposite situation; they are below the average standards of prosperity in Canada and they feel that if they cannot get into the economic mainstream there is no point in keeping the country the way it is. Then in central Canada, in Quebec especially, you have the French-English problem; we have the federal-provincial tensions; there are many difficult problems. But I have no reason to believe that we cannot solve them. If we look once again at the countries of the world, the new countries, the developing countries, which are made up not of true linguistic communities but sometimes of seven or eight or nine tribes speaking different dialects which have to form the same state – many of them have to borrow the language of other continents, French or English, to communicate amongst themselves within the same country – our problems are relatively easy. If we cannot solve them, if we cannot learn to have a strong and unified country in spite of our many ethnic origins, in spite of our wealthy and disparate economic regions, then I do not think Mr Ball should have any hope for the future of the world. If French and English, if East and West, if North and South in Canada cannot live together, how does he expect the Soviet Union and the People's Republic of China and South America to live with the United States? To me he is destroying his own case when he is applying it to Canada. Canada has problems but our problems are relatively simple. We have a very highly educated people; we have politicians who we hope will get better and better all the time; we have a great future and it is as great for us as it is for any country in the world.

Kitchener Chamber of Commerce, Kitchener, Ont., 21 May 1968

At Campbellton, N B, May 1969

This Canada of ours is a bold experiment. An experiment that must continue on orderly lines as it has in the past. Order is not stagnation. Orderly change need not lead to any less imaginative or desirable results than would the plans of those who press for precipitate reform.

Bold plans are no less bold because they are thoughtfully conceived.

Broad change is no less broad because it is carefully designed.

Orderly change will permit us to retain our sense of direction, our unity, and our diversity. Our unity must be of commitment to a better Canada, a Canada in which all the diversities which give us strength flourish for our betterment. A Canada in which the dignity and worth of every individual is protected; where each person is given an equality of opportunity which is real – unfettered by disease or ignorance or poverty. A Canada which exists as a free country in a world where freedom and peace are the norm, not an elusive target.

There have been some aspects of Canadian life which we have more felt than seen. Of these, the most evident and undoubtedly the most important, is the spirit of tolerance and goodwill which is an invaluable Canadian characteristic. Canadians take for granted what so many persons elsewhere seek and envy: human relationships that by and large accept without question differences in colour or origin or language. I stated on July 1 that we seldom reflect how fortunate we are in this country that there is a notable absence of bigotry and prejudice. Events of the past few weeks, however, have demonstrated that we cannot afford to assume smugly that these hateful characteristics are strangers to Canada, and are always absent. Nevertheless, if all Canadians are not yet able to live in dignity, by far the greater number of those who don't, suffer from indifference – not from hate; from neglect – not from prejudice. Not here do we find repression clothed in the guise of liberty, or violence tolerated in the name of law and order. This spirit of tolerance is our greatest gift, Mr Speaker; we must cherish it and never take it for granted. Against it we can judge our stature as a country and as a people.

But tolerance is only of benefit if it remains a positive force.

It is evil if it becomes an excuse for inaction or lack of care. Canadians must never become tolerant of poverty, of lawlessness, of suffering. Through their representatives in this place they must continue to make known their desire to share in the task of eliminating these evils, and we here must not flag in our attempts to find solutions.

House of Commons, 24 October 1969

If Canada's strength is in her people, her vigour is in the future toward which Canadians have turned instinctively for centuries. I personally do not share with any acuteness the sense of regret expressed by some commentators that Canadians pay insufficient heed to their past. The past we must understand and respect, but it is not to be worshipped. It is in the future that we shall find our greatness.

I think one point is certain, and it is that Canada appears when looked at from abroad – I admit I sometimes have occasion to do this myself – to be not so much a magnificent expanse of geography or a cluster of surging cities; rather it appears as people. Canada is Canadians. The great strength of this country lies in the good nature, the good sense and the goodwill of her men and women. Often, when we see this country from far away, we realize this. We see Canada as others see us.

One of the most touching tributes which was given to our country in this respect was paid by Queen Juliana of the Netherlands, when she told her children that they would like Canadians because they smiled easily.

To be vigorous and forward-looking is not enough to guarantee our future, however. We will be called upon to look upon it with imagination, to approach it with spirit, to plan for it with boldness. Daily problems will always be with us, but the government is not permitted the false luxury of concentrating only on the moment at hand. ... Governments must deal as best they can with current difficulties; they must discharge as well the responsibility of preparing for the future. This government accepts that responsibility. We shall continue to lay before Parliament the product of our planning. We seek a future over which Canadians will exercise some control, not a series of events by happenstance. Canadians have demonstrated in the past their disenchantment with governments which careened with uncertainty from one crisis to the next.

Exciting as that erraticism might seem to those who are stimulated by the froth and foam of uncertainty, it is not the choice of Canadians. We are called upon to work toward a secure and independent Canada within a peaceful world; a Canada in which social justice and economic growth are norms which apply to the lives of men and women in all parts of this country; a Canada situated within a harmonious natural environment; a Canada in which all Canadians take pride becasue of the opportunities available to them to participate in its governance and to contribute to its unity. That kind of Canada, that kind of future, we believe in, Mr Speaker, and we believe the Canadian people find it truly exciting.
House of Commons, 9 October 1970

Canadians by and large tend to think of Canada as a land of immense potential. Not just as a big land, which it unquestionably is. Or a privileged land, as many others enviously regard us. But as a land of limitless promise. A land, perhaps, on the threshold of greatness.
Toronto & District Liberal Association, 3 March 1971